f**k it
DO WHAT YOU LOVE

f**k it
DO WHAT YOU LOVE

John C. Parkin

HAY HOUSE, INC.
Carlsbad, California • New York City
London • Sydney • New Delhi

Previously published in the United Kingdom by Hay House UK, Ltd., 978-1-78180-246-5

Library of Congress Control Number: 2015953597

Tradepaper ISBN: 978-1-4019-4747-7

1st edition, January 2016

Printed in the United States of America

'Don't cut the person to fit the cloth.'

'For the first time in the human experience, we have a chance to shape our work to suit the way we live instead of our lives to fit our work… We would be mad to miss the chance.'

CHARLES HANDY – IRISH AUTHOR AND PHILOSOPHER

CONTENTS

THE 'YES, BUT...' CONTENTS

As I was writing this book, whenever I mentioned to people that I was creating a F**k It take on Do What You Love, I'd get one of two responses:

1. 'Wow, great, I need that! When's it coming out?' (Answer: *now*.)

2. 'Yes, but...' (and they would then reveal their perceived block on doing what they love).

So I started collecting all the number twos and made sure I addressed them in the book. Here they are, with where to find my response to them:

'Yes, but no one can just do what they love – grow up.'
(*Back to the short and hairless era*
in 5. Living By Doing What You Love; *see p.152*)

'Yes, but I have no idea what I love.'
(*Creating a 'What I Love' journal*
in 3. Find What You Love; *see p.66*)

'Yes, but what about money? My passion is acting,
but I need a steady income to pay my mortgage, bills, etc.'
(*Finding the money* in 4. Do What You Love; *see p.126*)

'Yes, but I have to think about everyone else in my life.'
(*Finding the money* in 4. Do What You Love; *see p.126*)

'Yes, but what if doing what I love makes me sick?'
(*Because you'll be healthier* in 2. Why Do What You Love? *See p.50*)

'Yes, but what if no one wants the thing I love doing?'
(*Go implement*
in 6. Making A Living By Doing What You Love; *see p.237*)

'Yes, but what if I do it and it doesn't work out? I'll have
nothing left to dream of.'
(*Instead of thinking 'either/or', consider 'both/and'*
in 4. Do What You Love; *see p.129*)

'Yes, but my parents wouldn't approve.'
(*Finding the courage* in 4. Do What You Love; *see p.99*)

'Yes, but it's hard to take a commercial or business approach
to doing what I love.'
(*Turning what you love into an idea that could earn money*
in 6. Making A Living By Doing What You Love; *see p.205*)

'Yes, but I might find out that I'm not good at doing what I love.'
(*Turning what you love into an idea that could earn money*
in 6. Making A Living By Doing What you Love; see p.205)

'Yes, but I could never make a living from doing what I love.'
(*I make a [good] living from doing what I love*
in 6. Making A Living By Doing What You Love; see p.192)

'Yes, but work is meant to feel difficult;
it's not meant to be like play.'
(*Play your way to doing what you love*
in 4. Do What You Love; see p.131)

'Yes, but I'd never want to work for myself.'
(*Being your own boss: it's brilliant/shit*
in 6. Making A Living By Doing What You Love; see p.197/199)

WHY THE EGG?

Why the fried egg on the cover, Parkin?

I spent two years pondering the cover design for this book (on and off, clearly: I didn't work full-time on it for two years). And then I pictured this fried egg and it just worked: I didn't quite know why. Sure, the egg could represent certain things that people might love – like cooking, or eating the food they grew up on, or leaving their job and becoming a chef.

The egg is a miraculous thing: a whole and wholesome food that arrives in its own packet. And it's also the most versatile ingredient in the kitchen. I was doing something I really love yesterday – wandering around Waterstones bookshop in London's Piccadilly – when I saw a book by Michael Ruhlman called *Egg*. It sits by my desk now.

In it, Ruhlman writes: 'The egg… is the Rosetta Stone [an ancient Egyptian tablet that helped us decipher a little-known language] of the kitchen. Learn the language of the egg – understand completely this amazing and beautiful oblong orb – and you enter new realms of cooking, rocketing you to stellar heights of culinary achievement.'

It seems to me that, like the egg (and the Rosetta Stone), 'doing what you love' unlocks the secret language of life itself. When you learn how to find your flow – and then to trust it, and follow it – everything starts to work. Real magic starts to happen when you're doing what you love. It changes your brain waves (to the more relaxed alpha ones), and as a result, you're happier, you're healthier, and you seem to recruit invisible forces that make everything work more smoothly.

If you're open enough, following the flow of doing what you love can take you anywhere. It's the most versatile of life-compass tools – just as the egg is the most versatile of ingredients. Doing what you love doesn't mean acting in a particular way, or following a set of rules, or leaving a job, or staying in a job, or persisting with something, or giving something up... it just means doing what you love. Whatever that is, in the moment.

By learning to Do What You Love in this book, you'll have your own recipe for a deliciously led life.

MY DOING WHAT YOU LOVE (OR NOT) AUTOBIOGRAPHY

I've looked back through my life and recorded the moments when I was doing what I loved (and also when I wasn't). It's actually been very enlightening to do this: a little bit like seeing your life flash before you, but with this filter on: *Did I do what I loved?*

You can write your own Doing What You Love (or not) autobiography. Get an idea of the times in your life when you've done just what the hell you've wanted to. And when you haven't. The times when you've said F**k It and done it. And when you haven't.

As you think about your whole life in this context, there will be some very obvious milestones that pop out. You don't have to go through your life and your decisions year by year — just get a sense of when these milestones were.

Here's my Doing What You Love (or not) autobiography — so you can see how I did it.

1971. I was a young boy, and early one evening I was dropping stones into a drain on the street where my family lived. As I dropped each stone, I'd watch it hit the water a few feet below, and then I'd imitate the sound it made by saying, 'plop'.

Suddenly, one of our neighbours – a rather severe senior policeman – appeared behind me. He simply pointed at me, and then walked away. I still wake in the middle of the night sometimes, wondering what it was I'd done 'wrong'. I was doing something I enjoyed, and it was judged (I think). Not a great start to a life of doing what you love.

Lesson: people might judge you for doing what you love.

1983. I'd cycle to school every day with my friend Gareth. It was a good distance and at one point in our journey, we had to go down a path that forked into two paths – one of which went towards school (Long Eaton) and the other towards 'town' (Nottingham). Each day, we'd take the fork towards school. But then one day we stopped, nodded at each other, and took the fork towards Nottingham instead.

It was a huge adventure – a feeling of total freedom that you only get when you're escaping from something that's oppressive and prison-like. That was one of the few school days that I actually remember. In fact, it's the highlight of *all* my schooldays – not going to school.

Lesson: doing what you love, even if it's against the rules, could be the highlight of your life.

1985. I decided to give up playing the guitar (something I thought I loved) to become a car mechanic (something I thought I *would* love), even though I had no experience of engines – or anything practical for that matter. While the other students went off to do their work experience in law practices and accountancy firms, I turned up at the local Ford car service garage.

It was hell. During my time there, the mechanics frequently joked about throwing me in the canal on my last day (which they said they did to all such temporary apprentices). The canal contained shopping trolleys, girders, rats and, probably, the dead bodies of previous apprentices, so as my work experience drew to a close, I was in a state of rising tension. On the final day, one hour before I was due to leave, I went to see the manager and told him I had a doctor's appointment, and needed to go. I then slipped out via the front door (the mechanics used the back door), never to see any of them again; and never to change the oil in a car engine again, either.

Lesson: finding what you love is a process of experimentation.

1986. I decided that going to university to do what I loved (which was reading great literature) for three years was probably a better idea than the alternatives (like working in the local Ford garage), so I finally got my head down and started studying.

Lesson: sometimes, getting to Do What You Love takes some hard work.

1987. I became a windsurfing instructor. Windsurfing was a passion of mine – and one reason I'd chosen a university located close to the sea – and I saw the possibility of a job as a windsurfing instructor after I'd graduated.

Lesson: it's fine to make plans to be able to Do What You Love for a living.

1989. During my final year at university I applied to management consultancy firms. Their salaries for new graduates were crazily high, and I'd also get to travel to the USA for training. I persuaded myself that it would be just the job for me.

Lesson: it's fine to play with all the options.

Later 1989. I declined high-paid job offers from management consultancy firms. One firm (Coopers-Anderson-Waterhouse-or-something) called my dad to explain how crazy I was being, and asked whether he could help persuade me to join them. Dad thought I was crazy too. But I wouldn't go.

Lesson: saying 'no', even when everyone is saying you should say 'yes', takes courage.

Still later 1989. I still needed some cash, so I worked for my dad's accountancy firm. It raised his hopes that I might stay on, and take over the business. But I was rubbish at it, totally rubbish — I couldn't concentrate on lists of figures for long enough. I left, which upset my dad, but I knew that it would all have ended in tears. This decision wasn't hard.

Lesson: not doing what you don't love is as important as doing what you do love. And sometimes people can get hurt in this process.

1990. I thought about becoming a combination of English teacher and windsurfing instructor in some unspecified-but-hot foreign land (I wasn't feeling too well, and my health tended to improve in the sun). But then I realized that was a crazy idea and instead went back to college (during a recession) to learn how to write TV ads.

Lesson: I should have taken my teaching-English-and-windsurfing dreams more seriously. I had a 'You have to settle down and get a proper job' thing running through my head. I could have ended up in just the same place (i.e. a hot place, next to the sea), and enjoyed the journey more, taking that route. But then again, who knows?

1994. I really liked the idea of a job that involved sitting around all day, thinking up ideas. And so I got my first paid job at a great advertising agency — BBH (Bartle Bogle Hegarty — they all still had acronyms back then) — on the back of a script for a TV commercial for Häagen-Dazs.

Lesson: I really wanted to work as a creative, but there were very few jobs around. So this was a real result. It came from sticking to my belief that I could do what I loved, and persevering with it through numerous internships, disappointments, and so on.

Later 1994. However, my heart's desire was to work for the coolest agency in London/the world – HHCL (Howell Henry Chaldecott Lury). They offered me a job soon after I started with BBH. And I took it, despite being sat down by BBH owner and ad guru John Hegarty, who told me I was making a serious mistake that I would regret forever.

*Lesson: It felt right. It **was** right: I had the time of my life at HHCL, where I was surrounded by genial geniuses.*

1997. I met Gaia. We did lots of stuff we loved – together. Not strictly Doing What You Love, but Marrying Who You Love.

Lesson: trust love, and trust instinct. Gaia is an angel and I'm a lucky man.

1999. I started to do something I love – using trance and shamanic techniques – while still working at HHCL. It became very popular and soon I was putting 20 or so people into trance a few times a week.

Lesson: sometimes you can incorporate doing what you love into your current life. It is possible.

2000. I began to work part-time, so I could do something else that I loved – screenwriting. Every Friday I'd put on my writing hat and write my screenplay.

Lesson: you might not have to leave your job to Do What You Love.

2001. I finished my screenplay. And as I pictured all the rewriting and agony required to get my film(s) made, I saw it would be another struggle. I just wanted to feel good in myself, so I decided to give up screenwriting and concentrate on the art of feeling good in myself: Qigong.

Lesson: always be open to re-evaluating whether you're doing what you love. Even if you have a well-mapped plan, don't be attached to it. Follow the passion, not the plan.

2002. Gaia and I packed up our London flat, climbed into a camper van with our one-year-old twins and headed for Italy: to look for a suitable bit of land and property on which to create a holistic retreat.

Lesson: it was crazy timing. Within a few days of leaving, we were crying in campsites. But we felt we had to get moving, so we did. Sometimes you can't resist the pull to Do What You Love.

2004. We opened our retreat, 'The Hill That Breathes'. It was tough at first, but a real blast. We were soon doing what we loved – living in an amazing place, hanging out with lovely people, and sharing ideas with them in a big tipi.

Lesson: getting to Do What You Love is often hard work. It might require sacrifices, and overcoming whatever obstacles are put in your way.

2005. We ran our first F**k It Retreat. Despite a lot of resistance from people who thought it wasn't a 'spiritual' idea, and that we were 'of the devil'.

Lesson: if you trust yourself, and Do What You Love, people may well resist it. But if it feels right, stick with it.

2008. I realized that what I'd really love to do is make music (again).

This became a struggle and a joy and a struggle and a joy for years to come.

Lesson: doing what you love is rarely plain sailing. I faced constant challenges, and the fear of making a fool of myself.

2012. We closed The Hill that Breathes in order to concentrate on teaching F**k It Retreats in various locations around Italy and the world. Despite the success of The Hill, we realized our real love was teaching.

Lesson: don't keep going with something just because it's successful. Success can make doing what you love even harder. We had to take a risk, make another leap, in order to stay on the track of doing what we love.

2014. Wanting to do less, and to stay at home more with my boys, I said 'no' to every single invitation that came my way: to talks and interviews and retreats and book offers. It gets easier to say 'no' after your first few.

Lesson: sometimes, to Do What You Love, you have to say 'no' to lots of things that you'd quite like to do.

F**K IT HELPS

We've been teaching our F**k It philosophy for 10 years now. And, over time, we've come to understand more about how using this profound profanity helps us. It helps in ways that other philosophies and techniques do not – it reaches the parts that other philosophies cannot, if you will.

Part of the reason for its effectiveness is the f-word word itself. Many studies now show the power of the profanity in various contexts, including its function in pain relief. For example, as part of a study at the UK's Keele University, volunteers (we hope) exposed themselves to pain by plunging their hands into ice-cold water, and were then given a variety of means to help them withstand it. Those who chose to repeat the word 'fuck' over and over again found it worked a treat, because swearing releases the body's natural analgesic.

The F**k It philosophy has also really helped thousands of people to relax, and take life less seriously. In fact, the other part of the reason for its effectiveness is its flexibility. Because, as well as helping us to 'let go' (as in 'Ah, F**k It, enough of this'), it can help us do the opposite, and 'go for it' (as in 'F**k It, I really want this').

F**k It helps us when we're stuck – it helps give us the push we need. Sometimes that push is in one direction (say, to do less) and at other times it's in the opposite direction (say, to do more). In the context of 'doing what you love', then, this means F**k It is a super-effective technique as it provides the 'push' that's required in whichever direction you need it. After all, if you feel you could do more of what you love, it most likely means that you're somehow stuck (in doing what you *don't* love). So F**k It will help 'push' you out of that 'stuckness'.

All the ways in which F**k It can provide the required push are detailed throughout this book, but a particularly potent summation of the 'F**k It Push' is the 'F**k It Push Mantra'. When we combine the words F**k It with an appropriate mantra – such as 'I can do it' – it adds the extra push needed. So, if you're scared about starting a new project, the F**k It Push Mantra 'F**k It, I can do it' would really help.

And a mantra, as you probably know, works through repetition: by saying it over and over again you can create powerful effects (just as our ice-water-plunging volunteers felt the benefit of the simple mantra, 'fuck').

Here are the F**k It Push Mantras I use in this book:

'F**k It, I can change this.'

'F**k It, I've had enough.'

'F**k It, I will face the facts.'

'F**k It, I can't stick this lot.'

'F**k It, no thanks.'

'F**k It, this just feels right.'

'F**k It, this just feels wrong.'

'F**k It, life is short.'

'F**k It, I can do what I love.'

'F**k It, I deserve it.'

'F**k It, I can do it.'

'F**k It, I must do it.'

'F**k It, it's now or never.'

'F**k It, no more excuses.'

'F**k It, I don't need this'

'F**k It, I will have my cake and eat it.'

'F**k It, I embrace this as it is.'

'F**k It, I can enjoy this.'

'F**k It, who cares if it's wrong?'

'F**k It, I'm fine making mistakes.'

'F**k It, all there is, is here and now.'

'F**k It, I'm happy to do nothing.'

'F**k It, what do I fancy?'

'F**k It, it doesn't matter so much.'

'F**k It, the money will come.'

'F**k It, do the figures.'

'F**k It to the rules.'

'F**k It, I'm off.'

'F**k It, I can make this work.'

'F**k It, who cares how good this is?'

'F**k It, who cares how good I am?'

'F**k It, it can be easy.'

'F**k It, I'm doing this for me and no one else.'

'F**k It, I will do this, one step at a time.'

'F**k It, I will make this happen.'

'F**k It, I need help.'

'F**k It, I'm happy being different.'

'F**k It, I won't do what I don't want to do.'

'F**k It, I will sing my song.'

You won't be able to miss these F**k It Push Mantras throughout the book, as their design is based on those 'Home Sweet Home' embroideries that you're probably familiar with (if you're not, Google 'home sweet home embroideries' and go buy yourself a kit).

INTRODUCTION:
LEADING A LIFE OF
QUIET DESPERATION

*'Most men lead lives of quiet desperation and
go to the grave with the song still in them.'*
HENRY DAVID THOREAU, *CIVIL DISOBEDIENCE AND OTHER ESSAYS*

Doing what you love. Simple, ain't it? As simple as boiling an egg? Well, no, if it were that simple, surely we'd all be doing what we love – all, or at least most, of the time? (Lots of commas there: I LOVE commas.)

But we're not; at least not us men. The American author and practical philosopher Henry David Thoreau suggested that it's most 'men' who 'lead lives of quiet desperation'. So does that mean he observed the women going about their daily chores with zest and vigour, all chirpy and gay? Were they singing with full voice a popular ditty of the time, while the men moped around, glum and desperate, but at least 'quiet' about it?

Or did he really mean both 'men and women'? I think the latter. Though I do get the problem here: 'Most men and women lead lives of quiet desperation' just sounds weird. It also begs the question, 'Don't we have a collective noun for the "men and women" thing?' To which we reply, 'Yeah, "people"'.

But 'Most people lead lives of quiet desperation' leads you down another avenue, doesn't it? Did old Henry observe the animals of the field, all chirpy and gay, going about their daily business with zest and vigour, while the 'people' moped around, glum and desperate, but at least 'quiet' about it?

Maybe — because many of us *are* leading lives of quiet desperation. We might not talk about it and admit it to others (that's the 'quiet' bit); we might not even admit it to ourselves (that's the fucked-up bit). But many of us are pretty desperate, and that's what living by not doing what you love (or like) does to you: it makes you miserable.

And there are also many of us who aren't really 'desperate', but still know that we're not really doing what we love (or like) in our lives, most of the time. We get on with it. We make do. We do our duty. We get by. But where's the joy, the passion? That's not a great situation either, is it? F**k It. Let's change it.

F**K IT, I CAN CHANGE THIS.

This F**k It Push Mantra: Although the natural pull is often to repeat patterns and to fall back to default mode, our brains are 'plastic' and life can be plastic too. When change is required (and desired) repeat this mantra for powerful results.

A year ago I was feeling desperate, so I created a quick emergency process and that relieved things quickly. In this introduction I'm going to share how I was feeling, and explain the process I used, but you'll also see that the deep work and the deep changes can take a while — which is why this is a whole book, and not just this introduction.

I'm writing this in March 2015, so we'll jump back now to the notes I wrote a year ago, in March 2014.

HOW DID I GET HERE?

I've been contemplating this book, hovering around its subject, for more than a year now. I realized recently though that it would involve more than noting down my ideas about how we can all do what we love. Sure, I've generally been pretty good at doing what I love, and making a living from it – after all, I sit here, looking out over the Italian hills on a Sunday afternoon, doing what I love, which is making a living from writing and a whole bunch of other things.

But… But… bloody but.

For a variety of reasons, some of which I understand and will explain, and some of which I don't yet understand, but will, and will explain… F**k It: I'm in a bit of a bloody mess.

Here goes: I'm knackered; I've got way too much to do; I'm not sure how we're doing financially; I'm not actually enjoying quite a lot of what I do; I lost my temper with the boys this lunchtime, for almost no reason; I've just got too many ideas, and I'm having trouble giving up any of them; I'm getting so many invitations to do things, and I've not, so far, been very good at saying 'no' to them; I've not kept myself as fit

> *F**k It: I'm in a bit of a bloody mess.*

as I could have – I haven't done as much Qigong as I would have liked – or been as careful with my diet as I should have been. And all because I'm just so bloomin' busy.

I've been trying to work it out, to prioritize – to sort out the one big thing I do every day, to give more time to my family – but it's not really working… I spent this morning, a Sunday, trying to eat into the 130 emails that have accumulated over the two days I wasn't able to look in my inbox (because we had a journalist and a photographer here doing a feature on us and our home).

And that's just a summary. It's not that I don't enjoy my life. I do. In fact, I spend a lot of my time rather over-excited and speedy about all the things I want to do. Like a kid high on M&Ms who's trying to build a city out of Lego on a 1:1 scale. Behind this Word document I have two stock videos downloading that I want to use to create a video for one of the songs – *It's Only Love* – on the EP that I'm hoping to release in about 10 days' time. 'Hoping' being the operative word, as I have a pile of other things to do too.

My office is a mess. My head is a mess. But the priority lists in my notebook attempt to navigate through this mess, so I know the things that I REALLY HAVE TO DO every single day of this week. As well as keeping on top of that constant inpouring of emails, and helping launch the update of our original F**k It book – which is out tomorrow, actually. Oh, and write *F**k It is the Answer* – the deadline for which is the end of May.

F**K IT, I'VE HAD ENOUGH.

This F**k It Push Mantra: When you've had it, you've had it. Face it. Admit it. And watch the space for movement opening up.

Oh, and help ensure that we keep it all fresh on our main business, F**k It Retreats. Oh, that reminds me, I must do that new video for the retreats, as I have all those great video testimonials from people that I took last summer. Oh, that also reminds me: I have all those audios that we recorded of everything we did last year, which we could turn into an amazing e-course series.

Are you starting to get the picture? My head is either in full-on creative mode, in which case a typical minute looks like this:

Creative mode

Why is it that women are now happy to apply their make-up while travelling on the Tube? It's kind of intimate, isn't it, doing that on the train? Would they be happy if I were to shave, with a razor, while sitting on the Tube? Then again, It's happening, so let's roll with it.

They should put mirrors inside Tube carriages, to make applying make-up easier to do. It would create a great advertising opportunity too: for cosmetics companies and manufacturers of hair products, and moisturizers… the whole lot of them.

Maybe it would make *all* our lives better if we had more time at home in the mornings to sleep and watch TV, and left the boring getting-ready stuff to the commute, rather than just standing or sitting there, staring into space or reading.

Actually, I'd prefer to have my breakfast on the Tube, if it wasn't so squeezed on there. They could have whole carriages as breakfast bars, serving fresh (squeezed) orange juice and croissants and muesli. Again, they could get sponsors and they'd make a killing. They really are missing a lot of tricks, that London Underground lot.

Each train could have some carriages for eating (breakfast, or other meals later in the day), and others for getting ready

5

for the day, with mirrors and make-up dispensers, sinks and shaving equipment.

Then they could have carriages just for reading, with comfier chairs. And some that are just for those people who listen to music too loudly on their headphones while nodding stupidly and occasionally mouthing the words. They could have other themed carriages too, including ones you'd sit in when you fancy a moan – those would contain lots of people who want to moan about stuff, including how few carriages there are devoted to moaners.

And how about carriages for dreaming about holidays, with sand on the floor and deckchairs for seating (these would be sponsored by holiday companies, of course). Oh, and... Oh, your minute's up.

Or my mind is in full-on organization mode, in which case a typical minute goes like this:

Organization mode

I really don't want to do those expenses from the London trip, but I must. So, I tell you what, spend an hour trying to get through the urgent emails, then an hour on the expenses; then you can spend an hour doing what you really want to do today, which is that music video... But I know that the emails are just too much, so why not rewrite the automatic reply?

Change the current one – 'John usually takes a couple of days to reply, please be patient' – to this: 'John only replies to emails once a week, and that day varies, so it might be tomorrow, or it might well have been yesterday, in which case you have about six days to wait. Though of course if it's really urgent, just reply to this email with the words "It's bloody urgent" in the subject heading and we'll endeavour to get a message to John. That might involve a pigeon or it could just be an old-fashioned telephone call, you never know.'

Shit, is it possible to enjoy any of this? What if I answered every single email with love, with a groundedness, with a sense of peace and purpose? Hold on, do those two go together – 'peace' and 'purpose'? Total bollocks, if you ask me. Just bloody well do the work – get on with it, and we'll sort out the peace bit another day.

So here I am. Too much to do. Not enjoying a significant proportion of it, but still probably enjoying it more than your average office-cubicle-wage-slave-jobsworth does. And I'm enjoying this: listening to deadmau5 (a Canadian DJ) rather loudly as the boys sit downstairs – probably watching horror films. And it's gently getting dark, and the words are being written. But it's not ideal, is it? I need to work it out. And this time, my reader friend, I'm going to work it out with you sitting there watching me.

You see, I normally write these book things like this: I spend ages organizing my thoughts and ideas and then I create a structure, even down to a list of chapter headings. I then head off to hotels and caves and things and lock myself away for short bursts as I write the thing. That allows me to concentrate fully and pour out quite a lot of words in quite short periods of time. And it's coherent because I'm full-time concentrating. I'm not distracted by the normal nonsense of everyday life (see above).

But for this book, I've found myself in this pickle. A pickle that, I guess, many of you are in too. And I want to get myself out of this pickle with you sitting next to me, watching how I do it.

This will be 'Live F**k It'.

This will be 'Live F**k It'. And I'll be doing that, with you, over the course of the next year (yes, my deadline is one year from now – I extended it as I knew turning my life around in such a fundamental way needed some time). Of course, there is the chance that I can't work it out, in which case it's unlikely that you'll be reading this book. I will have gone to my publisher and said, 'I can't work this one out, I'm fucked. Here's your money back, bye.'

But I guess, given that you *are* reading this, I must have figured it out, and turned it into a rather pleasant journey for both of us... a journey of discovering how to do what we love, and keep doing what we love, while still earning enough money to keep food on the table and the kids in decent clothes.

WHERE THE HECK IS 'HERE' ANYWAY?

During the walk I went on earlier this afternoon, I struggled to find the right metaphor for what I'm facing at the moment. The obvious one was being in a flooded room, trying to get the furniture out of the water. Trying to keep my own head above the floodwater, and trying to actually enjoy the movement of my body in it.

That metaphor came as I realized that one of the most important things I need to do at the moment is to stop stuff coming in. I've been inundated (a word which, as you may know, means overwhelmed, as if in a flood) by stuff. So, stopping the water from flowing in is the first step, and then I can start to get the water out, and dry things off, etc.

But that metaphor doesn't really work, because the flooding of my life in any way is not a pleasant image. And it's not an accurate reflection, either, because I do enjoy much of what I do. It's just there's so much of it, my enjoyment of the individual stuff is being reduced because of the volume.

An aside here, before I reveal the metaphor that did start to work for me – the one I reckon might work for you too. I find things much easier to do when I have visual images for them. It might only be me, but I think not. You see, our unconscious mind works more in imagery – you only have to look at the way our issues are 'visualized' and 'dramatized' in the world of our dreams.

A visual image is more tangible and easier to work with than simply writing things out. I can write out that I have too many things going on – I can list those things – but when you see the visual metaphor I came up with, you'll start to see how much more effective it is.

So this visual metaphor, or dramatization, of my current issue, is rather close to home. Remember, I'm trying to find a way to understand fully this mess that I'm in. It is, after all, only by fully understanding stuff that we can hope to begin to find solutions to the mess.

This is it: I imagine I'm sitting behind my desk in my office (that's still how I spend much of my working day, although there are times when I'm not literally sitting behind a desk), and that all the things that are taking up my time are personified as 'characters'. I then draw those characters and 'engage' with them.

Populating the metaphor

Let's start easy – this morning I'm sitting behind my desk in my office and there are three 'characters' with me. I've quickly sketched them in the first drawing (by the way, I'm sharing my rough sketches with you – that way you get to see that you don't have to be an artist to make your own scribbles).

Let's see who these three 'characters' are. From left to right, the first one is this book, about doing what you love: he's the man playing with flaming torches (that's my current idea for the book's cover, though who knows whether it will be the final design). In the centre is the many-headed email man. And the third character, the one with the TV head, is the video man. Now I'm ready to engage with them.

This morning, though I didn't really want to engage with email man, his heads were so numerous, and he was so noisy, that I decided to sit down with him. My fear was that, if I put off talking to him until tomorrow morning, he'd have sprouted many more heads, and I would certainly not have had the time to deal with them all. Once I'd sat with him for a few hours, he was calmer and could move to the back of the office, sit down and relax.

Next, I was really happy to turn to the video man for a little while. I searched through a stock video directory, trying to find videos that would help dramatize the idea that 'behind everything, is love'… I had this idea of a crowded urban scene that was very fast, but also very beautiful and very colourful – thus conveying the idea that underneath every aspect of a fraught and busy environment, there's beauty and love.

I found two videos that I liked, and downloaded them; now they sit waiting for me. I've allowed the video man to go and sit down at the back of the office too, but I can't wait to engage with him again. I may well do that later this evening, when the boys are in bed. You see I'm happy to hang out with the video man late into the evening, in a way I don't really like doing with the many-headed email man.

Then we come to our fire-wielding do-what-you-love guy. I'm actually really enjoying being with him now. It seems like just the right time. It seems exciting, and it seems therapeutic. As well as fulfilling a 'work' brief – I have to write this *F**k It – Do What You Love* book over the next year – it's helping resolve a HUGE tension within me: that of being submerged by this problem and not knowing what to do with it.

Starting to take action around the problem, in this case by hanging out with fire man, is actually beginning to relax me.

So, have a go at this yourself: 'personify' as characters all the stuff you're facing right now. You can include personal things if you want. I'm keeping it to 'work' things for now, but of course we have a whole range of other personifications, as well as actual persons, competing for our time each day. So go grab a notebook, or use your tablet in drawing mode, and get drawing your own room of characters.

You can draw your characters any way you fancy – look how elegant mine are – but maybe you'd like to incorporate a symbol to help convey what they represent. If, for example, you need to spend a lot of time today preparing a birthday party for one of your kids, then draw a kid holding a cake. The more work the drawings can do on their own – without your having to explain them – the better, and the more likely it is that you'll be successful in reducing your own workload.

Once the stuff of your day is personified in these characters, then you can start to engage with them. For example, as you address the 'task' of birthday party preparation, think about whether you can get any help. With making that cake, perhaps?

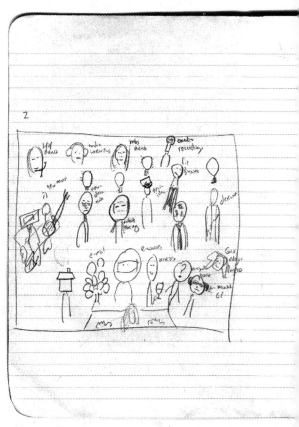

Right, I'm going to have a go now at visualizing all the other people and things that are demanding my attention at the moment – in these first few months of the year – in the context of my work time. I'm having to draw a big office, as there are a lot of them to fit in. (Yup, I'm doing this live: I told you I'd go through the process with you sitting next to me… I'm literally typing this and then drawing in my 'Let's Do What We Love' notebook.)

Oh crikey, I've just spent 20 minutes sketching all the 'characters', and my office is already full. Even though I drew a large one. Blimey, no wonder I'm tired.

Here's a guide to who's who in the second drawing. (Remember, we're personifying tasks as well as people here, so this drawing features personifications of the tasks, or projects, that I need to do.)

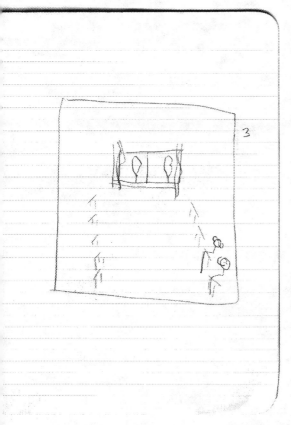

Back row, left to right

Hay House events. I normally do a few of these in a year, and they involve a great deal of preparation. For the last one, I prepared videos for a half-hour presentation. The preparation, and then being away for the actual event, takes about a week in total, full-time. As I said, no wonder I'm tired.

Radio interviews. These are fun, but it takes time to prepare for them. And then they drop a little grenade into my daily schedule.

Mind body spirit and holistic events. I speak at a variety of events every year, at venues all over the place.

Audio recording. I record a variety of stuff for a variety of purposes – for use in e-courses, or just to store ideas that are on my mind.

Middle row, left to right

New music. That, though you can't tell from the drawing, is me holding a guitar in the studio, with my producer mate at the mixing desk. I've spent a lot of time – my, a lot of time – in that studio in the last few years. Loved every moment, though.

Near-death book. A totally gorgeous idea I have for a fiction book. No, I'm not telling.

Robot therapy. A totally gorgeous idea for something else. Mum's the word.

Train idea. Now this is a fiction idea I've had for a few years. And it's a huge 'write it over 10 years' idea.

'F**k It Business'. For a while now, I've wanted to explore how F**k It can work in business. It will happen one day, won't it?

The money side. That guy with the currency symbols on his face is the character that represents everything on the money side for me – mainly sorting out our accounts.

The detective. That's another fiction book. Well, two actually. They're great ideas, but they may well remain as thoughts in a dark corner of my brain that only see the light occasionally – and most likely only when I mention them to someone else. If that 'someone else' is an up-and-coming TV producer, then I'm in.

Front row, left to right

See that house? It's The Hill That Breathes, and what we do with it is often on my mind.

The many-headed email man. There he is, the cheeky fella, sitting right in front of me again.

E-courses. That chap's wearing a space helmet because it's the symbol I'm currently using for all things internet course-y. I have many, many ideas for this. Let's see how many space men I can launch.

Retreats. My, he looks happy, holding that glass of wine. Retreats are what we do, much of the time. And I like them, I really do.

'Angels' book. What? I'd do a book on angels? Hush hush.

Music EP. That dude wearing earphones is listening to my EP… yes, the one that I've recorded, but not yet made videos for, or put out there for people to buy.

Gaia's Magic Projects. That's Gaia there – ahhhh – and she's a magic therapist, healer and teacher. There are so many things we could do with her magic.

So – WHAT TO DO?

Lock the door to the 'office'

This is the equivalent of trying to stop more water from flooding into my already flooded office. I need to say F**k It and turn away the two groups who are trying to get in:

Group A

These are the external people who come to me with offers and briefs and tasks. So, for the time being at least, I'm going to say a polite 'no' to anyone who wants anything from me: a speaking engagement, a radio interview, an article for a magazine. This is hard to do, as naturally I'm worried about missing opportunities.

Group B

These are the internal characters who crowd into my office in the form of ideas, and the projects that pop up in my head every day. I've known some of these for a while (some of the fiction project ideas, for example, have been around for years), but many tip up in my office every day, and ask to sit down and share a drink. They then proceed to get me a bit tipsy on the excitement of their proposal.

Yesterday, for example, I had an idea that I believe would be very exciting for my publisher, Hay House, involving music. It would be a big thing for their business. It would be a big thing for the world, in a way. But it would take a huge amount of time. And I currently have no way of judging all these 'people' in Group B who are sitting in my office – there's no way to distinguish between them, apart from who's shouting the loudest.

So, for now, I need to say 'no' to them too. This is even harder to do than it was for Group A, as it involves calming down the manic creativity that inhabits my brain cavity. But I have a plan, a cunning plan. Coming up…

Create a 'waiting room'

This is the cunning plan. I'm going to create a 'waiting room' just outside my 'office'. And, instead of saying: 'I will never do this project – I'm throwing you away', I'll say: 'Currently, there's no time available to give your project the attention it deserves, so if you'd like to wait over there, read a magazine about something you're not interested in, I'll be with you when the time is right.'

Having locked the door to prevent new people and things from coming into the office, I now want to gently shoo most of those who are already in there into my comfortable waiting room. We'll probably do this again later, more deliberately – choosing who to keep in the office, and who to put in the waiting room (and who to throw out altogether). But right now, the office is so busy, I can't hear myself think, so let's do this quickly. You can do the same with your room of characters.

So I'm drawing my waiting room and inviting people and things in there.

And this is where I stopped writing (and drawing) on that day. In fact, as you'll see from the third drawing, I didn't get very far with filling up the waiting room with those characters.

The next set of notes I found were written a week later...

So this is how the new system worked for the last week: I'd like to say things were less stressful, less busy, but in fact I've been very busy and at times very stressed. I've also been incredibly productive.

Let's look more closely at what happened. The good news is that I had increased focus – having shunted all those characters into the waiting room, I managed to really get down to it this week. I made and uploaded to YouTube those music videos – yes, THREE in one week. So I'm now pretty close to being able to release the EP. I also made a big step forwards with another project I'm working on. So 10 out of 10 for productivity with this new system.

BUT, I was really busy – and at times pretty stressed. And I'm feeling very tired after a full-on week. Why? Well, the energy I suddenly felt around doing the videos meant I was spending every spare moment on them – often working late into the evenings. It was fun, and I enjoyed it, but the email man's heads were becoming more numerous all the time. So, yes, the email man was very active – I was clearing emails one day, then getting another 60 or 70 within

24 hours (and that was after our office had selected just the ones that I have to deal with).

I said 'no' to invitations to do four separate events: a radio interview, a guest blog, writing a testimonial and writing an article for a leading magazine. (*We'll go into how to say 'no' later in the book.*) I was using my three-track mail system too – which allows me to separate easily what's urgent and what's not.

However, a few unexpected things threw me off track. There was a sudden rush to clear a new F**k It advertisement for the London Underground, on a deadline I hadn't been aware of. There was a rush of emails over the course of two hours, as everyone scrambled to get the ad working. But things got worse as more people became involved.

'Fk It, It Doesn't Matter So Much' is a key F**k It subject.**

There was a support issue too. One of our key staff unexpectedly missed a day's work, when she was needed – so I had to divert some of my energy. By Friday evening I had to close the email inbox and go for a 90-minute walk to clear my head and shake out the stress I'd accumulated.

Ah, and there was something else: as a side effect of clearing the 'office', I had some great new ideas. Here's one: 'F**k It, It Doesn't Matter So Much'. I realized that this is such a key F**k It subject, it could be a short book in its own right. On Tuesday, I didn't open any emails, and instead I sat with my breakfast and wrote furiously until I had completed that book. I then read it back, and it's good. I'm off to see the designer next week, to turn it into a little PDF e-book-like thing.

I've also resisted all attempts at editing it — sometimes the quick, energetically written stuff is the best. (*Note added later: you can read that actual book — just go to* www.thefuckitlife.com/dowhatyoulove)

Conclusion after one week of using the system: it was very effective, but still tiring and stressful. The system needs adjusting.

BACK TO 'NOW'

And so, back we are, one year later. Well, a little more than a year actually. Let me change out of these italics, but just so you know, this is one-year-later me.

It's actually amazing to sit here now, and read these notes; to hear the desperate me of a year ago, and to realize how much things have changed. And how different I feel. I'm not just saying this — as in 'Oh, look how effective this process is, and this book, too!' If I hadn't read those notes again, I don't think I would have remembered where I've come from.

So that's probably a good idea for you — to brain-drain how you're feeling at the moment. Just write and write, with no punctuation and no worries about grammar or sense — just write as quickly as you can, so the truth comes out.

Clearly, my fundamental problem back then was having too much to do. And the overwhelming quality of that volume cast a shadow over the whole range of work that I was doing. So even the stuff I should have really enjoyed was affected by that volume.

I've made some drastic changes over this past year, as you'll see when you read the rest of this book. I've become very good at saying 'no'. So my 'office' has really emptied out; and as for that waiting room — well, I haven't really invited any of the characters in there back into the office yet. I've also really calmed my over-creative tendencies, so I don't keep refilling either my office or the waiting room.

When I recently did the 'Do What You Love' exercises that are coming up soon for you, it was a completely different picture to a year ago. It was shocking to see. I found there was so much more that I loved in my *present*, and I struggled to think about new things that I might love in the future. My emphasis has switched from predominantly work to a real balance between work and home life (though as I work from home, it pretty much comes down to how much time I spend in different areas of the house!).

I'm at home most of the time now, because I've said 'no' to every single invitation to do things elsewhere. I'm even teaching half the usual number of F**k It Retreats this year (we do these close to home, so it's not even about travelling).

So, overall, as I'm seeing now (peculiarly, in this 'introduction': sorry for the jumping around), I'm much happier and I'm certainly not 'desperate' — as I was before. I have a really good balance. And I've found and developed some really great methods for reducing the amount of time I spend on what I don't like so much, and increasing the time I spend on what I do like. It works.

Sure, there are still things that are in progress. I've learned that real change takes time. You have to take one step after another. For example, I have things planned for the next six months that continue this positive direction (we're moving to the coast; I'm taking on a project manager to make some sticky projects happen; I'm toying with the idea of not having a fixed office, and so on).

And I'll mention this too: one of the first things I wrote in those notes last year was 'I'm not sure how we're doing financially.' That was a big stress for me. Having closed our thriving retreat business two years earlier (the physical retreat centre of The Hill That Breathes, that is – where we employed many people and ran retreats back-to-back. We still teach retreats, but in other venues), I'd slackened my control over the finances.

It was a reaction to my conscientious and almost compulsive keeping of the accounts for that business. So, with a smaller business, I thought I could do without such fastidious accounting attention. But I went too far the other way. And, as those notes suggest, one year ago I was really struggling with the stress of not knowing how things were going.

I'm right next to you, working out how to fix things, the F**k It way.

Later last year, I finally got down to working on the accounts. It wasn't a pleasant job and it wasn't a particularly pleasant picture. But it was a great relief to finally *understand* what was going on, and that understanding of the issues also helped me fix them. Quickly.

So I want to welcome you to this journey. I also want you to know that I'm not sharing these ideas about how to Do What You Love from a distance. I'm sitting right next to you, feeling the same pain, and working out how to fix it, the F**k It way, day by day.

And, like no other book I've written, I sense the *importance* of the subject of this one. I feel I have a great responsibility here – to share with you ideas that work, and also to impress on you the urgency of sorting this out: we need to get living a life in which we do what we love, as much as we can.

I

ARE YOU DOING WHAT YOU LOVE?

'Musicians must make music, artists must paint, poets must write if they are to be ultimately at peace with themselves. What human beings can be, they must be.'

ABRAHAM MASLOW, US PSYCHOLOGIST

I was in a band when I was a teenager; many teenagers are. Paul was too, and he loved it. But he'd left school at 18, and being in the band wasn't going to pay the bills. He was being hassled by his dad, Jim, who kept saying: 'Satan finds work for idle hands.' He told Paul to go out and get a job. 'I've got a job, I'm in a band,' said Paul. But his dad said: 'No, you have to get a proper job.'

So Paul went to the employment office, and they sent him to a company called Massey & Coggins, who were looking for someone to sweep their yard. He took the job, but before long a manager said to him: 'We can't have you sweeping the yard – you're management material.' So Paul then had a steady job with prospects.

But then one day, two members of Paul's band dropped by the factory and told him that they had a gig. Paul said that he couldn't join them, because he had a steady job now. It paid well enough, and he was also being trained, so he couldn't expect any more.

Paul was serious about not going with the band members, but then he thought: 'Sod it, I can't stick this lot.' He jumped over the wall and went to do the gig. And that gig was at The Cavern in Liverpool. And Paul McCartney never went back to Massey & Coggins.

F**K IT, I CAN'T STICK THIS LOT.

*This F**k It Push Mantra: Think of your favourite Beatles song when you say this one. Or Wings' Mull of Kintyre, of course.*

Maybe if Paul had stayed with Massey & Coggins and become a manager — if he'd led a comfortable life with a happy family and children and grandchildren — and we'd been able to interview him (when he was 64, say) and ask him if he was happy and whether he'd done what he loved, maybe he'd have said 'yes'. And meant it.

He seems like a naturally positive and happy man. Maybe he would have been just as happy, maybe not. But I don't know whether the rest of the world, over the last 50 years, would have been. I'm also struck by the fact that Paul McCartney, in his decision to leave that job, used his own version of F**k It — 'Sod it'.

F**K IT, BE HONEST – ARE YOU DOING WHAT YOU LOVE?

You don't have to tell anyone the answer to that question. You don't have to say it out loud. You certainly don't have to tell me. Or Paul McCartney. But — are you doing what you love? Really?

I ask this because most people are not (and they are probably leading lives of 'quiet desperation' as a result, as we've seen). But most wouldn't admit to it: to others or themselves. And that's a problem.

You see, admitting that you spend most of your precious time on Earth not doing stuff that you love, is something of an admission of failure in this life thing, isn't it? And most of us don't want to be failures, do we? We want to be successes, in one way or another. So we feel we're successful if things are going well in our career (even if we hate the work), or if we have

F**k It, be honest with yourself.

a nice house (even if all we do is sleep in it) and a nice car (even if we just drive to work in it), or if we have a family (even if we rarely see them).

Ah well, at least we've got some letters after our name, or some numbers in our bank account, or some more lines on our CV… it's just that the letters l-o-v-e don't appear much in there. Yup, most of us don't really spend that much time doing what we love. Oh, how evolved we are.

F**K IT, I WILL FACE THE FACTS.

This F**k It Push Mantra: When you sniff any denial in yourself – any 'going unconscious' (which includes watching endless amounts of TV and eating too many snacks) – take the smelling salts of this mantra, and determine to face the facts, however unpalatable they may be.

Don't feel like a failure if that's the case with you. But do, please, F**k It, be honest with yourself. No one knows. No one's listening.

And if you told them, they'd only say, 'Oh, you're not a failure – you have a great job, family, etc., etc.' Because they too are afraid that they're failures and are not leading a joyful life.

Being honest with yourself – with *ourselves* (I can't leave myself out of this) – is one big step towards changing this state of affairs. And I'll say it now – it's not so easy. Sure, some bits of it *are* easy, but filling the majority of your time with stuff you really love is not so easy. And even when you manage it, there's a danger that you'll stop enjoying it after a while anyway.

Knowing that something is wrong

As you know, just over a year ago, I realized that I was no longer loving something I'd been investing quite a lot of time in – doing speaking gigs and events. It wasn't that I was doing hundreds of these, but more that the ones I said 'yes' to would take up a lot of time – what with the preparation, and the travel, and so on.

I told myself that I liked doing them. Or rather, I told myself that the final bit – standing up there and touching people (not like that), and people liking it and applauding, and then the relief of going back to the hotel room and lying down – was worth all the rest of it (the weeks of preparation, the days of rehearsal, the nerves before going up on stage). Oh, I also thought that the extra publicity for F**k It, and being out there with people, made it worth it too.

But underneath, I knew there was something wrong. And then a couple of things happened that made me resolve to get off that stage, and sit at home more, doing what I love (tapping away on a keyboard like I am now, and then hanging out with my family downstairs – watching movies, playing board games, and so on).

One of these things was an email I received from an organization I was due to speak for. And here it is – with the bits that might identify them taken out:

Subject: ACTION REQUIRED – THANKS :-)

To: The F**k It Life

Hello John,

Your talk with us is coming up soon, yay :-)

Can you put the word out about your ███████████████ ███████ talk in social media and on your website? :-)

And if you could send two – or more :-) – messages to your list. How big is your list?

I've included banners that you could use for your social media and on your site: ████████████████████ ████████████████████

And please do make sure you 'like' our Facebook page. :-)

If you could tell me please once you've done all that too, so we can promote your ██████████████████ talk further.

I look forward to seeing you soon,

Best,
████████ :-) xxxxx

Now, no matter how many smileys and kisses there were in that email, it made me feel hassled, and hassled is the last thing I want in life. I like to do my own thing, at my own pace, with my own people.

And the fact that I'd somehow got to a position where someone thought they could happily (smiley, smiley) hassle me reminded me that this game wasn't for me.

I was just about okay if people lauded me (and paid me well, too), but the line between it being tolerable and being intolerable was too narrow. When you do something you love, you can put up with a lot of nonsense in order to carry on doing it. But when the love levels are lower, it doesn't take so much to knock you out.

So, after a couple of jolts like that, I sat down with myself, and a nice cup of tea, and asked (myself):

* *Do you love this?* No, not really – just some bits of it, but they're not worth it. And I'd prefer to be at home, actually.

* *Is there any way you could do the bits you like without the bits you don't?* Errrm, well, yes, if I only did events that I organize myself. I like those more anyway, and no one can hassle me.

* *Is there anything you'd lose by not doing these events?* Maybe, yes: some traction, some publicity… but F**k It, I just don't want to do this.

I thought, F**k It, I just don't want to do this.

So I stopped. And then, just to test me, I got even more invitations to do gigs – from all over the world. And I've said a polite 'no' to them all. Even the ones that tempted me (South Africa and Istanbul, since you ask). I've had a much better year as a result, but that's only one part of it – more on that later. So I was honest with myself, and I invite you to do the same.

F**K IT, NO THANKS.

*This F**k It Push Mantra: Keep saying it, so you
get used to it. Get the universe accustomed to
the idea that you can, politely, say 'no'.*

Aha, interesting. Lovely timing this…I just paused to look at some emails, and I saw a newsletter from my mate, and fellow Hay House author, David Hamilton. He's talking about the upcoming Hay House 'I Can Do It' event, and mentioning some of the great authors who'll be speaking there. But this year my name isn't on that list of authors, as it normally would be, because that's one of the many things I said 'no' to.

Funny feeling, this. It's the effect of saying 'no' to things, and you have to anticipate it. Saying no has its downsides. The question is, are the downsides more than compensated for by the upsides? As I think of my boys downstairs, currently doing their homework, and the time we'll spend together later in front of the TV, or play-fighting, or on the trampoline, the answer is… YES.

So, it's time to flick on your honesty field, and answer the following questionnaire. It will help you find out how much you're doing what you love.

i.

Overall, **how much** do you **love your job?**

(Do you wake up raring to get on with the job, or is it just a pay cheque?)

little 1 2 3 4 5 6 7 8 9 10 lots

ii.

Overall,
out of work hours,
do you manage to
do what you love?

	1	2	3	4	5	6	7	8	9	10	
not really	○	○	○	○	○	○	○	○	○	○	yes really

iii.

How many things
are there that
you'd love to do,
but don't?

1 2 3 4 5 6 7 8 9 10
○ ○ ○ ○ ○ ○ ○ ○ ○ ○

iv.

When you were young,
were you doing
what you loved
more or less
than you are now?

1	2	3	4	5	6	7	8	9	10

less ◯ ◯ ◯ ◯ ◯ ◯ ◯ ◯ ◯ ◯ more

v.

Can you imagine
a situation
where you're doing
significantly **more** of
what you love
than now?

1 2 3 4 5 6 7 8 9 10

not
really ○ ○ ○ ○ ○ ○ ○ ○ ○ ○ oh
yeah

WHY DO WHAT YOU LOVE?

Aha, here's a beautiful coincidence: as I write this on a Sunday morning, the boys downstairs doing their homework (all right, probably playing on Playstation), I'm also listening to *The Archers*. For those of you who don't know it, this is a long-running BBC radio soap opera set in a rural village, and today two of the characters are talking about our subject. Look, I know *The Archers* is not the most F**k It of shows, but read on…

Here's the briefest of backstories, so you understand the bit I recount:

Husband and wife David and Ruth run a farm called 'Brookfield' that has been in David's family for generations. A proposed new road will cut the farm in half, so, after months of agonizing discussion, the couple have decided to sell up and move to another part of England, where

*Admittedly, The Archers is not the most F**k It of shows.*

they'll be closer to Ruth's ailing mother. They have a buyer who is offering a lot of money for their farm, and they intend to buy a new farm in the new location.

But then, very late in the process, David began to doubt their decision. He found a toy farm that he'd played with as a child, and it reminded him of his family's deep connection to the farm. He suddenly realized that he and Ruth can't leave the farm: he just *knows* it. But now he has to tell Ruth (and that's what I'm listening to now, live).

Ruth has just asked David why he's changed his mind about the move. And David replies that it's a 'gut thing': that it's who he is. He says that the land and the farm are who he is and who *they* are, and that this has always been the case, through good and bad times. Ruth asks whether they can talk about it, but David is insistent that they cannot leave. His feeling is so basic, he says, and he knows that leaving Brookfield would simply be wrong.

Ruth is not happy, but David goes on to tell the buyer that they've decided not to sell the farm after all. Interestingly, David had begun to feel ill and exhausted as they neared the completion (closing) date on the sale (his mother had noticed this, and later said that if the couple *had* moved, it would probably have killed David).

So, in this *Archers* storyline, we have a few elements relevant to this very chapter about why we should do what we love:

* David became sick and exhausted after a critical decision had been made. This is often a good indication of whether a decision, or a route we've taken, is right for us, and consistent with doing what we love.

* David talked about his decision being a 'gut thing'. The couple had discussed the pros and cons of the move, and had looked at all the rational arguments for months, but David knew now that it was beyond rationality – it was about gut instinct. Knowing whether something is right for us goes way beyond the brain cavity. It often takes a long time (as it did for David) to realize and understand what we really want and need.

* Whatever appears to be good 'on paper', can just feel 'wrong' in the end (and David did describe it as 'simply… wrong').

And that reminds me of all those people who introduce their situations with variations on this: 'It's all good on paper. I've got a great job – it pays really well, and it's what I've always wanted to do. But… but it just feels wrong.' Sadly, we don't live our lives on paper. It would be a lot simpler if we did (though rather more dull).

F**K IT, THIS JUST FEELS WRONG.

This F**k It Push Mantra: When the feelings fight with the thoughts, use this one to give the feelings a knuckle-duster.

Ah, another coincidence. Leonard Nimoy died a couple of days ago. He played Mr Spock in *Star Trek*, and as a 'Vulcan', he saw everything purely rationally. But we're not Vulcans, although sometimes we act as if we are. That's a great invitation for us to balance our emotional and rational sides, isn't it: *We're Not Vulcans, You Know.*

Right, let's get down to this chapter, which should start with a brilliant quote.

WHY WE SHOULD ALL DO WHAT WE LOVE

'Man is truly great when he acts from passion.'
Coningsby – Benjamin Disraeli

Oh dear, that's another quote that makes me think, *What about women then, eh, Disraeli?* He dressed like a girl, anyway.

So Why Do What You Love? Why eat delicious food? Why laugh at a good joke? Why embrace those you love? Why go on holiday to sunny, beachy places? Why drink enough to get a little bit tipsy? Why buy that gorgeous pair of shoes? Why desire that beautiful person in the bar? Why go to the cinema and sit with a bucket of popcorn in your lap? Why walk barefoot in the park? Why wear those sunglasses that make you feel cool? Why lie in the bath 'til your digits go wrinkly? Why read a book 'til way past bedtime?

Why read bedtime stories to your kids? Why wander round art galleries looking at paintings? Why listen to your favourite music? Why sit by a real fire in your local pub? Why go sledging when it snows? Why go swimming in the river when it's hot? Why go to the best restaurant you can afford? Why get a Chinese takeaway (again)? Why linger in the biscuits aisle of the supermarket? Why lick the plate clean? Why sleep in on a Sunday morning? Why gossip with your mates?

Why Do What You Love? Because it's what you love, stupid. And…

Because life is short

F**k It, life is short. Most of us don't know how many hours we'll have on this planet. And whether we live a relatively short life or a relatively long one, most of us conclude that our stay on Earth is actually quite 'short'.

Of course that judgement is subjective. Our life is long compared to that of some creatures. For example, a mayfly lives for anywhere between 30 minutes and a day. But mayflies make up for what they lack in longevity with quantity, and intensity, as their primary function is to hatch and reproduce.

If humans had the lifespan of a mayfly, we'd be born in a (rather large and over-busy) hospital early in the morning, spend the morning growing up, the afternoon fucking, and the evening fading away before dying at midnight. 'Not a bad life,' I heard someone in the audience mutter. Goodness me.

F**K IT, LIFE IS SHORT.

This F**k It Push Mantra: In the armoury of F**k It Push Mantras you have to assist you when you need courage to do something beyond your comfort zone, this is the Kalashnikov.

Of course there are people who perceive life differently, as a bit of a drag, and they might say that it feels far too long, actually. Clearly if you're suffering deeply, life may well feel as if it's too long. But, for most people, life feels short. Especially once we're getting on a bit. Time does seem to accelerate as we age.

"""""""""""""""""""""""""""""""

I said F**k It and left my comfort zone – with a job, husband and house – and moved to a new city to become what I'd always wanted to be: a writer and a coach. Although there have been bumps along the way, so far it has been the best journey I have ever been on. For the first time I know what freedom feels like.

VERA MUENCH – HEILBRONN, GERMANY

,,,,,,,,,,,,,,,,,,,,,,,,,,,,,,,,,,,,

Our boys, now nearly 14 years old, are currently talking a lot about when they were 'really little': they mention songs that they recall listening to; they remember family holidays, and how they used to dance to Michael Jackson in front of the guests at The Hill That

Breathes. They remember all this as ancient history, saying: 'Do you remember, Dad, back when we were little, when we used to…?'

And I *do* remember, but it feels like yesterday. No, that's not true: it's just an expression to convey this very thought, isn't it? It seems like very recent history to me though. My grandma used to say 'It feels like yesterday'. As she faded away, in her 80s and 90s, she didn't really understand how she could still feel 21 on the inside, while everything was very different on the outside.

We fill our lives with stuff to get through… but for what?

So when we say 'life is short', it feels true to most of us, and we know what it means: given our limited time on this planet, we should really make the most of it, eh? We should, really, savour every moment, as that's all we have, isn't it? A long (but not infinite) series of moments: aka 'the present'.

Instead, what we do is fill our moments with stuff to get through: jobs to complete, hurdles to overcome, problems to solve… but for what? To finally achieve some far-off idea of happiness? To finally get away on that holiday? Or collapse in front of the TV over Christmas?

As you'd expect, Eckhart Tolle (author of *The Power of Now*) has something good to say on this subject: 'Most people treat the present moment as if it were an obstacle that they need to overcome. Since the present moment is Life itself, it is an insane way to live.'

Well said, Eckhart. We are, most of us, totally frickin' insane. But you don't need me, or Eckhart, to tell you that, do you? You know it yourself. And to prove it, I'd like you to do an exercise. Come on… this could be one of the most powerful things you do here.

It's time to write a letter or two

Grab a pen and paper. Actually, ideally, you should grab a pen and some traditional writing paper (for letters). If you don't possess such a thing any more, then normal paper will do. You're going to write a couple of letters.

The first one will be from the 17-year-old you to the present you. Yes, just imagine sitting down as the 17-year-old you, and sending some advice to the older (present) you. It might be along the lines of 'Just remember how it felt to...', or 'Please don't ever forget...'. Those are just pointers, though. The best thing to do is try to transport yourself back into your 17 year old brain, and get writing. Just go ahead and do that now.

I'll write mine now: from the 17-year-old me to the 47-year-old present me. But don't read mine yet – do your own first.

> Dear (older) John,
>
> I'm sitting here, John, in our study at school, with a steaming cup of coffee and the radio on in the background. You remember this study, don't you? And these moments of peace and freedom? I hope you've managed to find peace and freedom in your/our life. I've not enjoyed the slog here at school – the long, enforced march of this education. And I can't see us (do you mind if I call us 'us'?) doing what everyone says we'll be doing – becoming a solicitor or an accountant. Thank God for university.
>
> I'm not going to think too much about what comes next – I'll just get to university and see what happens. I hope we get to do what we want there. I hope we get to do more of what we want afterwards, too.

At the moment, I'm just concentrating on getting through…
but I'm really loving English literature (I can't believe I didn't
'get' it before)… and playing the guitar… and windsurfing…
and driving around in my little car. And my hope is that I get
to do just these things at university.

John, I'm writing this slightly nervously. I really hope it goes
well for us. I hope we're happy. I hope we don't get forced
into doing stuff we don't want to do, as has happened here
at school. It's funny, the idea of passing a message to you/us –
but if it's anything, my message is: 'Try to avoid getting stuck,
and try to do what you'd like to do.'

All the best, John: I hope it's good for us.

Johnx

Next, write another letter, from the 77-year-old you to the present
you. (By the way, I chose 17 because it's a critical age – that 'almost
adult' time. And I chose 77 because it's old enough, but not so
ancient that you'll have to imagine yourself croaking from a hospital
bed. I didn't realize it when I chose those ages, but I am, at 47, exactly
between those two points. What a funny thought: that 77 is as far
ahead of me as 17 is behind me.)

Okay, old man John: please write your letter to present John.

Dear (younger) John,

And you thought you were getting old? You should try it from
here. Nooo, it's fine, actually. Like sitting on a hill as the sun
goes down – calm and gentle. I suspect you're glad to hear
that.

Well, the good news is that it all worked out fine. There are going to be difficult times for you, of course – I won't tell you any of the details – but you know that it's not always easy. But you (we) got through those, and learned from them. And I see this now from here – that things are never quite as bad as you think they're going to be. So you really can relax about everything – it does all work out.

Now I know (I remember) that you were full of life – and that you were excited about a lot of stuff – but also that you'd get frustrated too, and try to rush through things. Well, my message to you is to savour it all: to try to be present to it all… it's never perfect, and it's never completely in balance.

It's never really as you'd plan it, either – whose life is? So make all your plans, and adjustments, and have all your dreams. I know I can't stop you from doing that – but ENJOY IT ALL along the way.

I know you've done that before. I know you know how. And as you live each moment – from where you are now, to where we are here – sit back a little more and just enjoy the ride. Even if it's bumpy, just enjoy it. Because it's one helluva ride we've had here, boy (you don't mind if I call you 'boy' do you? What a granddad thing to do!). Maybe you don't see that fully now, but it really has been one helluva ride.

Love you, Johnx

I also asked our boys to write letters to their ancient 47-year-old selves. (That's funny: I just calculated the boys' age and they are exactly 13¾, an age that's familiar to me from my childhood – and to some of you, I guess – because of the fictional character Adrian Mole, whose first outing was in *The Secret Diary of Adrian Mole, Aged 13¾*. In fact, I've just looked it up, and Adrian is pretty much my age... So he'd be 47 now, too.)

Okay Leone, aged 13¾, off you go:

> Dear older me,
>
> (I mean, 'Dear even cooler older me'.)
>
> I hope you remember that money isn't the most important thing in life, and that you're doing a job you really like.
>
> I really hope you're not stressed. I hope you're not chubby, like my dad. I hope you have a family with some children... And that you're happy.
>
> Love, Leone

And now it's your turn, Arco, aged 13¾:

> Dear older me,
>
> I hope you're a brilliant and creative guy.
>
> I hope you're a director or a photographer – though I mainly hope you're happy.
>
> Please remember how imaginative I've always been. Remember how many ideas I come up with every day... and remember to never stop dreaming.
>
> I hope you're having a very, very good life.
>
> Love, Arco

Thanks, boys. Hopefully, as it did for us, this exercise will emphasize to you why it's worth Doing What You Love.

❝❝❝❝❝❝❝❝❝❝❝❝❝❝❝❝❝❝❝❝❝❝❝❝❝

My F**k It moment came two years ago, after my beautiful mum suddenly died from a rare neurological disease, CJD. I simply said, 'F**k It, life's too f**king short, so I'm going to live it fully every single day. This isn't a rehearsal!' So I'm doing just that now, and she would have fully approved.

LUCY COOTE – MONACO

❞❞❞❞❞❞❞❞❞❞❞❞❞❞❞❞❞❞❞❞❞❞❞❞❞

Because you'll be happier

I planned to use a quote from The Man I'd Often Like to Quote But Can't Remember or Pronounce His Rather Difficult Name, Mihaly Csikszentmihalyi (F**k It, I've just copy-and-pasted that bit from an article about him), so I've just been researching him (again).

And another nice little coincidence has arisen – after *The Archers* and Adrian Mole, this is clearly the chapter of coincidences – which is usually an indication that I'm in flow and things are flowing nicely. Relevant allusion to 'flow' alert…

So, the psychologist copy-and-paste Mihaly Csikszentmihalyi is most famous for his idea of 'flow'. While at the University of Illinois in the USA in the 1980s, he led some rather innovative research on happiness called the 'Experience Sampling Study', aka the 'Beeper Study'.

In previous studies, people had been interviewed, or had filled out questionnaires, about their levels of happiness in the past. But in the Beeper Study, researchers gave electronic beepers to 480 teenage students, and asked them to record their thoughts and feelings whenever the beepers went off – which was every two hours or so.

I found a newspaper article from the time, published in the *Idahonian Daily News*, which reported on this ground-breaking study. It found that the teenagers listened to less music than you'd expect (surprising), liked watching television less than you'd expect (surprising) and enjoyed least the activity of homework (not surprising). And the kids felt better doing sports than just about any other activity (maybe surprising, or not – depending on your view and experience of sports). The study also noted that the kids fell into stereotypical gender divisions, with the boys spending more time doing 'yard work' and the girls 'cooking and cleaning'; the girls were also much more concerned with their weight.

It seems that we are happiest when we're completely absorbed in our activities.

And that was it. From that article about the research (in which copy-and-paste Mihaly Csikszentmihalyi was not mentioned by the way – probably left out by a lazy sub-editor who didn't want to check the spelling of his name… You know, it really is amazing that this man has become so famous with a name like that, isn't it?), one conclusion that could be drawn is that we should 'get kids to do more sport'. And also, 'let's all do more sport', as it makes us happier.

But, copy-and-paste Mihaly Csikszentmihalyi's takeout from the research, and his famous idea, is that we are happiest when we are completely absorbed in our activities. When we are thus absorbed – whether in a sport or in a creative pursuit – we enter a state of consciousness that he calls 'flow'. During this 'optimal experience' we feel 'strong, alert, in effortless control, unselfconscious, and at the peak of our abilities'.

My 'flow' moment

Now – coincidence alert again – that research was being done in 1985, when I was sitting there in my study at school, as a 17-year-old, writing to my present self (well, sort of). You'll recall that I mentioned windsurfing in my letter, and it was while I was out windsurfing a couple of years later that I experienced the concept of 'flow' for myself. By that time I was at university, where I was much freer, and doing more of what I loved – including windsurfing at a nearby seaside town several times a week.

I actually remember the moment – as I was flying along on my board – when I realized I was really, truly happy (we don't remember that many actual moments of a thought process do we?). But it was a peculiar kind of happiness. Not a self-conscious one ('Ooohh, I do enjoy windsurfing: I'm happy'), but one where I was, for the majority of the time, entirely absorbed in the process of windsurfing.

I'd been zipping back and forth for a couple of hours, and I suddenly became aware that I'd been entirely absorbed by a range of requirements: to adjust the sail with my arms in relation to the wind, and keep adjusting it; to adjust the board with my feet as it passed over small, choppy waves, and keep adjusting it; to anticipate where to turn and prepare for the difficult manoeuvre of the turn; and finally to stay relaxed in my body in order to create more speed.

I did all this with an underlying, bubbling awareness of the exhilaration of flying along at speed – with the sea spray on my face and the sun beaming down on my… (Okay, I can't 100 per cent remember whether the sun was shining that day – I admit that the chances are small, but allow me some imaginative filling-in of the details.)

I remember thinking that this experience of 'happiness' was peculiar – particularly the element of it not being a self-conscious happiness – that the happiness really was arising from being completely and fully absorbed by the task of windsurfing, and that, for the period I was on the water, everything else disappeared.

Up to then, if I'd been asked, I'd probably have said that being happy brought along with it an *awareness* of being happy – for example, you're at a big gig, enjoying the show, and aware that this is a momentous occasion and that you're at a big gig and enjoying the show.

I'd probably have believed that sitting peacefully, looking out at a beautiful view, would make me happy, and self-consciously so: *Wow, what a view, aren't I lucky?* So I remember the slight shock of the perception that I appeared to be at my happiest when I somehow *disappeared* into this activity.

And that state of disappearing, and being fully absorbed, is what copy-and-paste Mihaly Csikszentmihalyi called 'flow'. In fact, this is what he wrote about it, pretty much around the time I was on the water (I like to think it was on the same day, in a moment of electrifying synchronicity): 'The best moments in our lives are not the passive, receptive, relaxing times… The best moments usually occur if a person's body or mind is stretched to its limits in a voluntary effort to accomplish something difficult and worthwhile.'

And that perfectly describes my windsurfing experience that day. My body *and* mind were stretched to their limits (yes, really, it was a windy day, and it was hard work) in a voluntary effort to accomplish something difficult and worthwhile. It was difficult, and I did also see it as 'worthwhile' for a variety of reasons: it was keeping me fit and well; I saw the worth in my total enjoyment of it; and I was considering windsurfing as a career option (as I was, by then, an instructor).

Back then, that insight was important for me. And there were other important lessons I learned on the water: such as the more you relax, the faster you go. I could never quite understand why, but an effort simply to relax my body more and just let go would make the board skim over the water even faster. And we *were* going fast: at that time, I was windsurfing alongside the then speed record-holder in the UK, so I knew I was going fast. And I could see small differences too, in the changes that I made.

You see how that lesson – the more you relax, the faster you go – has affected my life?

So, 'doing what you love' makes you happier. In this specific area of activity: doing something you love that entirely absorbs you. When we come to look at what you really love in your life, do bear this aspect in mind: think about the times and the activities when you just *disappear*. (It's also worth remembering what Mr copy-and-paste said about being 'stretched' in the body and mind: when we're noting down what we 'love' we should therefore not exclude the activities that really stretch us.)

The more you relax, the faster you go.

And, funny that, I've just looked at the clock and it's nearly lunchtime. Which is a real surprise. I really haven't been aware of time this morning. I've been so absorbed in this. And I'm really enjoying it. I have, clearly, been in 'flow'. Ladies and gentlemen, you're in good hands.

"""""""""""""""""""""""""""""""

I said F**k It and let life flow, even when it got really difficult and confusing. One year on, I've sold my house, resigned from my job, bought a VW camper van, and written a short story, which is being published. I'm now about to relocate to the south of France, to see what happens next.

JAKE MIDDLETON – LEEDS, UK

,,,,,,,,,,,,,,,,,,,,,,,,,,,,,,,,,,,

Because you'll be healthier

At the end of 2012 – soon after we all realized we weren't going to die in the apocalyptic scenes the ancient Maya had predicted – I read an article about an American woman who had actually just died. Not of the plague, or after being hit by a meteorite, though – just of old age. Her name was Midge Turk Richardson.

She was an extraordinary woman – she'd gone from child actress in Hollywood, to nun, to New York socialite – and so full of life (until she died, of course). And she was someone who clearly acted from great passion. (I'm remembering Disraeli's words, 'Man is truly great when he acts from passion' here – I'm not referring to her literal 'acting' but the way she conducted her life.)

Agnes Theresa Turk (known as Midge because of her short stature) was born in Los Angeles in 1930. As a girl, she worked as an extra in more than 100 films, occasionally opposite Shirley Temple. But when she was 18, she decided to turn her back on her buzzing life, and her boyfriend, to become a nun with the Sisters of the Immaculate Heart of Mary.

By all accounts Sister Agnes Marie, as she was known, thrived, and loved the life of service. But in her mid-30s she became frustrated with the church leaders' inability to meet the needs of the impoverished community she was working with. She became depressed and exhausted, and in the end, she actually went blind.

So in 1966 Sister Agnes Marie took the unusual step of asking to be released from her vows. And, as she made this decision to leave the order, she... wait for it... she regained her sight. She went on to lead a full life – she even edited the teen magazine *Seventeen* (there's that number and that age again!) from 1975 until her retirement in 1993. Under her stewardship, the magazine raised serious discussions about sex (one cover headline read 'What you *Must* Know About Herpes'), anorexia and suicide.

Your body and your mind know when you're doing what you love.

Midge Turk Richardson provides an extreme example of the possible deleterious effects of *not* doing what you love. She was clearly a vivacious (in the sense of 'full of life'), powerful woman who, when she wasn't able to do what she loved (i.e. help her community), actually lost her sight.

Your body knows when you're doing what you love, just as your mind does. And sometimes your body will tell you when you're *not* doing what you love. Sometimes, you can sense the effects in your body in the moment: if you're doing something that scares you, for example, you may feel butterflies in your stomach. But, if you're simply not doing what you love – generally, in your life – you might not see immediate physical ramifications.

Test how much you love something

Your body is affected directly – in the moment – by how much you're loving what you're doing. There's a method to test this, and it's called applied kinesiology or muscle testing. We use it a lot on our F**k It Retreats because it's a great way to dig deep into how we really feel about something – or to understand the effect on our bodies of certain thoughts.

The thing is, to perform the muscle testing, you'll need a partner. Not for any kinky stuff – the idea is to test the strength of your arm as you make certain statements, and you need another person to help you do that. If you want to try this at home – and it's perfectly safe – here's what to do:

Muscle testing

* Stand up straight and hold one arm out to the side. Ask your partner to stand immediately behind you. Begin the test by saying your own name out loud, repeatedly: e.g. 'I'm John, I'm John, I'm John'. As you do this, have your partner press down gently on your arm, at the wrist (as in the drawing).

* As you continue to repeat your name, and your partner continues to press down on your arm, try to resist that pressure and keep your arm raised. Then rest for a moment.

* Ask your partner how difficult, or easy, it was to push down your arm while you were saying your own name.

* Next, pick a name that doesn't mean anything to you, and repeat that in the same way: for example, 'I'm Fred, I'm Fred, I'm Fred'. Again, try to keep your arm raised as your partner presses down on it.

* Then ask your partner in which instance your resistance was the strongest. It should be that your arm is strongest when you're saying your own name.

You can test other 'truths' by using this test, if you want: just to be sure that it really does work. What you soon realize is that in your own arm, you have a lie detector. Your ability to resist – i.e. the strength of your arm – is a very good indicator of the truth (to you at least) of what you're saying. (If you now rush to your actual partner/husband/wife and get them to hold up their arm while asking, 'Do you fancy Cynthia/Fred at the office?', then slap wrist – and push down arm.)

More muscle testing

So, as we're on the subject of Why Do What You Love, have a go with that. Choose two things – one that you actually do love, and one that you don't really love, but think you should. Then construct two assertions from these two things. Here are some examples:

Assertion 1: 'I love sitting in front of the TV on my own, eating chocolate.'

Assertion 2: 'I love cooking healthy dinners for my family.'

(Aside: though you may be tempted to accuse me of lazy gender stereotyping here – plucking a housewife from the 1970s as my example for Assertion 2 – I actually plucked that from my own personal and present experience. See, I'm just like my mum after all.)

Have a go with other examples if you want. In fact, you can use this method to find out whether you *really* love something, or you're just kidding yourself (and others). Here are some examples of that:

'I love doing the housework, I really do'. *Yeah, right.*

'I just love being a primary school teacher.' *Yeah, right.*

'I love being the captain of industry that I am.' *Yeah, right.*

'I just love helping people – it's when I'm at my happiest.' *Yeah, right.*

'I love my husband/wife.' *Yeah, right.*

'I love the smell of napalm in the morning.' *Yeah, right.*

It's cool, the muscle testing, isn't it? You really do have a lie detector in your own body. In fact, it's not far off the *actual* lie detector test. Follow this logic, it's awesome:

A classic lie detector test – you know, the type that was used by retired CIA agent and prospective father-in-law Robert De Niro on Ben Stiller's Gaylord Focker in *Meet the Parents* – works by assessing how 'stressed' a subject is. The polygraph (lie detector) equipment measures stress by the level of electrodermal activity (EDA) – the umbrella term used for defining autonomic changes in the electrical properties of the skin.

The theory says that if you start to lie, your stress levels increase. If you're telling the truth, your stress levels don't rise. So, it's impossible to lie and stay relaxed. The muscle-testing method also measures stress levels. When we're stressed we become weaker. When we're telling the truth, we're stronger. So the old saying 'the truth makes you stronger' is literally true.

Muscle testing shows that you can use your body as a lie detector.

These observations and conclusions, if true (and just keep doing the muscle testing if you have any doubts – you could test me now and see that I'm telling the truth) have huge implications for your life. Follow this logic, it's awesome:

* Whenever you're doing something that doesn't ring true for you – that's not really 'you', that's not 'your truth', that you downright hate – then this 'lie', this dissonance, is occurring.

* When you're in this 'lie' and dissonance, it's not possible to be relaxed – as in the polygraph (lie detector) test. You will, whether you know it or not, be stressed (and the machine or the pressed-down arm will know it).

* It's stress in your body that can lead to ill health (and, conversely, relaxation that leads to healing). This has been observed in the realms of Western science and medicine, and it's the cornerstone of Eastern medicine, where a

discipline like Traditional Chinese Medicine observes that good health is reliant on the harmonious flowing of energy through the body, and such flow is reliant on (among other things) relaxation.

* This means that copy-and-paste Mihaly Csikszentmihalyi's 'flow' – where you are in your 'truth' – leads directly to relaxation, which leads directly to energy flow in the Eastern model, which leads directly to healing and health. Ergo, doing what you love is healthier for you.

So, it may well be that what you love is 'sports' – as those teenagers did – and that's good for you. But it may also be that what you'd really love is to leave your stressy city job that gives you a lorry-load of cash each year but not a lot else, and become a lorry driver. And that would be good for you, for your health. (Aside from the endless hours spent sitting behind a wheel, only sporadically interrupted by fat-and-calorie-loading stops at roadside cafés, and sessions in the back of your lorry with truck-stop hookers, that is.)

The moment you replace something you hate with something you like, it's like going for a long walk in the fresh-aired countryside. The moment you make the decision to stop seeing each moment as an obstacle, and start enjoying what you're doing, even *love* what you're doing, it's like sitting down to salad, with seeds and nuts (and whatever else you put on salads) – and not following it up with a bar of chocolate. No, Mum, don't.

Because you'll be more successful

I've met a lot of successful people in my life. I don't just mean successful in business – I've met successful actors, athletes, authors, poets, scientists, doctors, therapists, film directors, and so on.

And yes, I've met many successful business people, too: captains of industry, dot.com billionaires, city bankers who could have retired in their 20s, PR gurus, entrepreneurs, and so on. In my book *F**k It Therapy* I observed that the most successful people in any field tend to be relaxed – just think of Usain Bolt, Pele, Barack Obama, George Clooney and Richard Branson.

I've observed, too, that the successful people I've met share another quality: they LOVE what they do. There's always a twinkle in their eye when they're talking about their thing: it's clear that it's their passion. Often, money comes with the success, but usually it's not about the money for them (though sometimes, making money *is* their passion, so it is). These people had a passion for whatever their thing is when they first started out, before the money started to flow in. And they have this passion now.

All the seriously successful people I've met LOVE what they do.

I haven't met one seriously successful person who has not enjoyed his or her job or thing. I've not met one who got bored of it, or resented it. These people were living their passion, and their success meant they could make a living from their passion.

So, based on my own observation, it does seem that Successful People Are Doing What They Love. But does that also mean that Doing What You Love can make you a Successful Person? I think, generally, yes. It gives you your best shot at success – however you define that – in the area of your thing.

Why? Well, there are several reasons:

* **You're more relaxed.** Remember, doing what you love naturally relaxes you, and as well as keeping you healthy,

being relaxed has a huge impact on whatever it is you do. People are more inclined to be with you, follow you, *buy from you*... Also, situations are more likely to go well for you (imagine a situation approached by two people in different states: one stressed and uptight, the other relaxed and in flow).

In fact, the idea of 'flow' – although we're stretching its definition by the introduction of copy-and-paste Mihaly Csikszentmihalyi's idea – is that it extends well beyond your own body: everything is energy, and thus everything flows. By relaxing, we slip more easily into the wider flow – although that's a big (and possibly abstract) idea. More prosaically perhaps, because you're doing what you love, you're more likely to: get up earlier to get going; go the extra mile, and smile more whilst you're doing it; sacrifice more when necessary; inspire others to join you (or buy from you).

✳ It gives you a sense of 'purpose'. One that's as powerful in the present as it will be in the future. Your purpose is: *I'm doing what I love*, and *I'm making this work so I can continue to do what I love*. And purpose is powerful: it's your compass in whatever you do, and it keeps you on track. But a purpose that's pointing somewhere off into the future (for example *I want to bring peace to the world*), and is therefore composed of deferred gratification, is less powerful.

The tension of the purely future-pointing purpose – the discrepancy between where you are now and where you want to be – creates stress. And we know that stress is not good for anyone. The 'purpose' of doing what you love floats across time, so you're relaxed in the present but you still have your purpose-compass guiding you into the future.

So yes, Do What You Love, work at continuing to Do What You Love, and watch the success happen (partly because the 'success' has already happened, simply by your doing what you love).

Because you'll be wealthier

There's no bigger money magnet than passion.

(As an aside here, it's interesting to note that the industry of carnal passion, porn, tends to lead the money-making side of many an Industry or medium: in the early days of the internet, there was no bigger money magnet that the porn industry, and it will probably be the case when we finally get to some kind of virtual-reality experience of sex.)

Let's unpick this assertion. Money is a form of valuing things, obviously. I earn money because people have decided that they value what I do, and what I have to offer, which, in this moment, and beautifully cyclically, is talking about the value of money.

When I value what someone else has to offer (say, their skill with a pair of scissors, a razor and a hairdryer) I will express my valuing of their value with our chosen system of value attribution – i.e. money. I can create my value in your eyes in a variety of ways: I can be an authority on something; I can offer something that no one else is offering; I can offer something of value for less monetary value than others do.

I can even help you see value in me that you didn't know you needed (this has been the purpose of advertising for years: creating apparent 'needs' where there previously weren't any).

But the sure-fire way for you to understand my value is for me to totally love what I do. Yes, I'm more convincing in every way if I love this thing. But it's deeper than that — it's about the element of 'truth' that we explored earlier. When I'm doing what I love, all that I do arises from, and is bathed in, truth. This means that I am, in every way, authentic. And this isn't contrived authenticity — it's *authentic* authenticity. Contrary to what a salesperson might tell you, it's very difficult to trick people: most of us can spot — no, can *feel* — the difference between an authentic person/offer, and a contrived person/offer.

Imagine trying to sell something that you don't believe in. Even if you learn all the best sales techniques beforehand, and attend high-level acting classes, if you don't believe in what you're selling, then it's not you: it's not your truth. Remember the lie detector test — it's impossible to be relaxed in that situation. Whether you're relaxed or not will be picked up on by your prospect — whether they know it consciously or not. Truth is, you'd be rubbish at selling if you didn't believe in what you were selling.

So I've had you imagining selling something there, and you might be sitting there saying, 'Well, I'm not selling anything, so how does this apply to me?' But we're *all* selling something, in one way or another. We're selling our value to the world, and the world is replying by valuing our value with its chosen value attribution system of money.

Even when there's no actual money involved, we're still all in the value-exchange business. When you meet your new neighbours, value-bartering will be going on: you'll want to convey that you're nice and reliable, and might occasionally do them a favour, in the hope that they're nice and reliable and might occasionally do *you* a favour. And when you ask a policeman for directions (yes, it's 1950s Great Britain), you're value-bartering.

Even when you're buying, you're selling. For example, if I go to buy a new car at a showroom, I shouldn't kid myself that I'm just a 'buyer', as I'm also selling. I'm selling *myself*: I want to sell the idea that I'm a serious potential buyer (and thus worthy of their serious attention); I want to sell the perception that I'm a canny buyer and that therefore it'll be worth offering me a good deal; I want to sell the idea that I'll become a long-term customer and that therefore I'm worthy of special, consistent attention and treatment.

> *Nothing is more valuable than real, and nothing is more desirable than passion.*

So, even when you're buying, you're selling. And if you're always selling, then believe in what you're selling – whether it's yourself, or your thing. And the best way to believe in it, is for it to be what you love. If I do what I love, and love what I do, and live by doing what I love, and make a living from doing what I love, then I become a huge money magnet. Because nothing is more valuable than real, and nothing is more desirable than passion.

3

FIND WHAT YOU LOVE

*'All children are artists. The problem is how
to remain an artist once we grow up.'*

Pablo Picasso

This is where it would be easier if you were here with us, in Italy, on one of our retreats. We'd sit you down with a pen and paper and get you writing about all the things you love. I say 'easier' but it's actually just as easy for you to do it there, now, wherever you are. Of course, we can't *know* that you're doing it, but we'd really love you to, as it's a very illuminating process, and a fun one, too.

In this chapter, you're likely to find the key that unlocks the door to doing more of what you love in your life, and all the consequent joy, health, success, etc.

(That's a marvellous 'etc.' isn't it? As if added 'joy, health and success' wouldn't be good enough! It reminds me of a magazine I saw in our bathroom this morning – one which Gaia must have bought, I hasten to add – called *Livingetc*. I sat there for a while, trying to work out what the 'etc.' in its title could mean.

Surely *everything* concerning our lives and our time on this planet is covered by the word 'Living'? The only thing that's not covered by

'Living' is, of course, 'Dying'. So was this 'etc.' a euphemistic reference to Dying? I liked that idea: a magazine that covers 'Living & Dying' – yes, *everything* – really appeals to me.

So I picked up the magazine and flicked through it. But I couldn't find one reference to Dying – there weren't even any ads for life insurance or anything. So it looked like this was a magazine *just* about Living: there was no real 'etc.' at all. But that's still a very wide brief, isn't it? How could the magazine's creators begin to approach such a vast topic?

Well, it seems they'd concluded it was best to narrow things down somewhat, because most of the content was articles about the homes of rich people. For page after page I saw the very stylish, very tidy and very modern homes of people who could clearly afford to spend a couple of thousand pounds on a chair.

So I turned back to the cover to examine this increasingly misleading title a little more. And there I found a subheading [aha, the subheading]. It was in capital letters, but set very small: a mixed message if ever there was one. It was like a wizard putting a spell on someone to make them very, very small – the size of a mouse, say – but leaving their voice at normal adult amplitude, so the mouse-sized human could shout and scare the living daylights out of you, because it would be very hard to spot them.

Here's that small but shouty subheading on the magazine: THE HOMES MAGAZINE FOR MODERN LIVING. Aha: so it doesn't cover the over-ambitious subject of 'Living', or even 'Living etc.', at all. Instead, it's a 'homes' magazine [i.e. *We're going to show you lots of 'homes', but probably not the messy kind that you live in, otherwise why would you buy the magazine?*].

And it's for 'modern living', which has be euphemistic, doesn't it? I mean they're not excluding 'old-fashioned living' from their brief. They're not excluding those who insist on having no digital devices, or those who still have their loo outside in the back yard, or those who use a warming pan to heat their bedsheets in the winter, and keep a potty under the bed.

They're not even referring to common aspects of 'modern living', such as perpetual stress and anxiety, or the pressure to be so many things and successful at everything; or the startling and ever-increasing gap between the rich and the poor – to the point where you can walk a few metres down your average London street and see a dozen properties worth more than £3 million... and three people living on the pavement.

No, 'modern living', for them, means a slick, modernist interior design style. So 'Livingetc.' is actually *the improbably tidy homes of the 1 per cent.*)

Sorry, that was a lot to say inside one set of brackets. In fact, I had sub-sets of brackets in there too. Brackets within brackets: that's like a Russian doll of punctuation. However, I intentionally let myself go there for two reasons:

I. I've learned that making such observations like the one above, and digging into absurd detail, is something I love doing. Though we know it's clearly not the case, I love to imagine a meeting in which magazine people dream up the title of an ambitious new project that *will* cover Everything. One person suggests 'Living', and the others all go, 'Brilliant, brilliant.' Then someone says: 'But does that cover *everything*: is it really inclusive of the whole lot?' And then there's a pause before someone pipes up with 'Living... etc.'... and they all start to applaud. I love to share these fantastical asides with you occasionally.

2. You need to let yourself go in this stage of the process. You need to be able to dream and ramble and be absurd and consider the impossible.

CREATING A 'WHAT I LOVE' JOURNAL

While you're thinking about what you love, you'll need a way to note down your ideas, so we're going to create a 'What I Love' journal. I write in my journal periodically: when I feel like it, or when I feel the need to – which is usually when I've become stuck doing too much stuff that I don't particularly like. For me, keeping a What I Love journal is like a Doing What You Love recharge.

> *You need to dream and ramble and be absurd and consider the impossible.*

Each time I do the journal, it brings up some really interesting stuff that invariably bounces my life off in a different direction – sometimes dramatically, sometimes more subtly. It was doing such a journal back in 2008 that made me realize so clearly that I wanted to be making music (again). And that realization has had a huge impact on my life and my time (and my bank balance).

I would recommend using a notebook for your journal, as the pages of a book give you a lot of flexibility – and the option to draw, too. You can use a digital device of some sort if you prefer. But I wouldn't. When I do the journal, I mainly write, but I also doodle. Okay, so I can't draw very well, but I still like to doodle.

So I'm going to give you a glimpse into my world of 'What I Love' because a. you'll really get how to do this journaling process, and the range that's possible with it, and b. I fancy doing it again, and I think it will help me take you through the steps.

I'm both excited and slightly nervous about doing this. And maybe you're feeling that too. I kind of want to look, but also don't – as I'm scared of what I might find (i.e. that a dramatic, new and irresistible direction might appear out of the pages, and bounce me off what I was thinking was my current Do What You Love thing).

Please please please please please please please do the following exercises yourself. Please. They are so simple. Please don't censor yourself while you do them: just write out your responses to the questions as quickly as you can.

My, there were a lot of 'pleases' in that last paragraph. But how else do I emphasise the importance of doing this yourself? I was brought up proper, so my only way is to ask nicely, and smile, as I invite you to sit down and start writing.

You also don't have to do all the exercises in one sitting; I carry the journal around with me when I'm doing them. And then add things as I realize I love them (for example: *Oh, I'd forgotten how much I love skimming stones over the surface of a lake with the boys*). Don't try to work out how you could do the things that come up for you, or do them more, or make money from them. We'll come to that later.

Exercise 1: What is it you love doing?

Okay, let's go with the first exercise. Ask yourself the following questions (in bold) and write down (and/or illustrate) the answers in your journal. I've given some of my responses to the questions as examples.

What do you love doing?

(By this I mean in your life at the moment, generally speaking.)

* Sitting on the sofa between Gaia and my boys – all snuggled up and watching *How I Met Your Mother*.

* Walking: in the hills near home; at the sea; in a local town; in London; day and night; short and long. I love walking.

* Driving: on my own, or with all the family. With all the family asleep, late at night.

* Writing down absurd observations.

* Coming up with new ideas for things.

* Making ideas happen.

* Being at the dinner table with the family. The rambling Italian. The struggle to understand. Then the bursting into English again.

* Having a bath.

* Swimming in a warm sea.

* Teaching people Qigong.

* Doing Qigong.

* Feeling relaxed to the point of bliss.

* Listening to music that makes me jump around.

* Making music that makes me jump around.

* Having new ideas for our business, and planning them out in minute detail.

* Having lunch and dinner with guests at the retreats in Urbino or Stromboli.

* Meeting guests that we haven't seen for years.

* Catching up with family, back in Blighty.

* Being on my own in London.

* Spending hours and hours in Waterstones bookshop, Piccadilly, London.

* Having a tidy office and a tidy house.

* And a clean car.

* Hugging the boys.

* Doing the washing-up with the boys.

* Going out for dinner with Gaia, on our own; the boys at home, on their own.

* Eating chocolate.

* Eating piadina (an Italian flatbread) at the piadineria in Fano (a coastal town near us).

* Reading in the bath.

* Reading on the beach.

* Seeing how people can make changes that will have a massive effect.

* Solving people's business problems in half an hour.

* Writing in that 'weird zone'.

* Getting through a to-do list.

* Having a pizza and a beer.

* Reading *The Guardian* newspaper on my phone.

* Following a football match live, but via 'updates' on my phone.

* Joking with the boys.

* Trying to work out the world with Gaia on our walks.

What did you used to love doing?

This can be from any time in the past – if you want, you can range from memories of childhood to things you've done in more recent years. Here are mine:

* Looking in rock pools in Cornwall, Southwest England.

* Sitting on trains and looking out of the window.

* Reading Philip Larkin's poems (about sitting on trains, looking out of the window).

* Playing football, with the garage door as the goal.

* Windsurfing.

* Painting little fantasy figures in the dining room while listening to an album by The Police.

* Lying on my back in the dark, listening to music through headphones.

* Cycling 'no-handed'.

* Playing the guitar.

* Playing hide-and-seek.

* Being on campsites.

* Washing the boys every morning.

* Driving down to university: the long, long drive on my own.

* Browsing in record shops.

* Browsing in bookshops.

* Getting ideas from weird magazines.

* Sitting high in the tree in our front garden, so no one could see me.

* Sitting around chatting with friends.

* Having nothing to do.

* Going to 'the carvery' for Sunday lunch.

* Watching Nottingham Forest football team play at home.

* Mountain biking in Black Park.

* Sitting on buses.

* Drinking with mates.

* The lead-up to Christmas.

* That amazing go-kart Anthony had.

* Playing video games in arcades.

* The Wagamama restaurant chain when it first opened, and you had to queue and queue to get a place.

* Cinema trips: arty, trashy, and *Blade Runner*.

* Licking my *Jaws* pendant.

* Licking pencil sharpeners.

* The feeling of a job well done.

* Believing I'd invented a massive new theory about Shakespeare.

* Dreaming about Dungeons and Dragons.

* Dreaming about playing lead guitar on stage.

* Playing truant and escaping on the last day of school.

What can you imagine loving doing in the future?

(This could be stuff you already do, or completely new stuff.)

* Travelling round the USA with the family.

* Driving a fast car round Europe with Gaia.

* Doing a massive F**k It gig.

* Working entirely from cafés in Fano.

* Walking on the beach for two hours every day.

* Going to New York for a few days.

* Doing Qigong on the beach every morning.

* Swimming in warm seas around the world.

* Walking the coastal footpath in Cornwall.

* Helping businesses and business people use F**k It to make big leaps.

* Reading my book *Bob the Buddha* to a theatre audience in London.

* Creating a *Bob the Buddha* 'museum' in a London flat.

* Holding hands with Gaia in 1,000 new places.

* Writing a fiction book.

* Writing twisted observational blogs that everyone reads.

Okay. Now, what you're seeing here is the written-from-the-hip stuff that I did in the moment. Remember, you can continually add to your own answers as you realize there are more things that you love.

What do you notice about your answers?

Don't do this too soon, but the next stage is to read through what you've written in response to the questions and see if anything really stands out for you.

What stands out for me is that I found it very easy to answer the first question (the 'present' one), but it was harder to answer the third question (the 'future' one). This is in total contrast to the last time I did the journal, when I had a huge amount of excitement about the future stuff, and all the things I could do.

I see that a lot of the things I love now are quite 'homey' things, and that's what I'm enjoying most at the moment – being at home with my family and going to the beach with them. As you know, I've made a lot of changes in the past year – I'm travelling a lot less, and have stopped doing talks and gigs, and I'm really loving that.

Our homey-changes continue this summer, when we'll move to Fano, a town on the coast, so that's why I'm looking forward to walks and Qigong on the beach. Doing the journal exercise, and writing this book, reminds me that I don't actually do enough writing, which is something I really love. I think blogging is the obvious outlet for that, so I resolve now to follow through on my plan to do two blogs at least once a week, for our regular F**k It readers and for business people too.

And on that note, something else has arisen for me big-time in recent months – the desire to work with businesses and business people again (it's been more than 10 years since I was doing so in a formal capacity). It feels as if this 'Do What You Love' project is a great bridge between F**k It in the personal life and F**k It in business life.

I've noticed that I'm now doing a lot of what I love.

Okay – can you see what I'm doing there? I'm noticing what's going on for me and what it's bringing up, and coming to some conclusions too. I'm seeing that I've actually changed quite a lot. I'm seeing that I have more changes in the pipeline – and that I'm now doing a lot of what I love – but there are a few relatively easy things for me to do, to slip more into that (like writing a regular blog).

So you can do the same – and do make notes as you realize things. As I said earlier, my biggest realization when I did this in 2008 was about the music: so answering the 'past' question in this exercise gave me great intentions for answering the 'future' question. I had a flood of ideas about what I could do, and you might be having lots of ideas now about what you could do. Write them all down.

Exercise 2: What don't you love doing?

On the retreats, at this point I'd usually go into more exercises to explore other things we might love doing. But first I want to flush something out. I know we have to do this now, as I feel it's missing from my own picture. I'm suddenly thinking, *Oh, my life is really cool — look how well I'm doing*, when I know that's ignoring some critical parts of the picture.

Never be so wedded to a process/plan that you can't veer off it.

So now we're going to look at the stuff in our lives that we don't particularly love. I've got a feeling too, that incorporating the dark side of the picture into the 'what do you love doing?' exercise might create some interesting fuel for the exercises that follow.

You see — I told you I'd be doing this live. I'm adapting the process as we go along, depending on what feels right, in the here and now. That's a trick you can use too: never be so wedded to a process or a plan that you can't happily veer off it occasionally.

Right, as you did in the first exercise, ask yourself the following questions (in bold) and write down (and/or illustrate) the answers in your journal. As an example, I've given my response to the first question.

What are you not loving doing, or even hating?

(Again, this is in your life, at the moment.)

* Getting the *Survival Guides* done, as they are so frustrating.

* Getting the right mix of design and designer and software for all our stuff.

* Working through the complications with the accountant.

* Sitting in my office for too long when it's sunny outside.

* Sitting down for too long, because I love moving.

* Working out what to do with The Hill That Breathes.

* Living in a messy environment.

* Struggling to find the right help.

* Struggling to delegate certain things.

* The one stuck relationship that I'm struggling to unstick.

What do you notice about your answers?

Okay, having done that, here are my quick observations and conclusions:

1. This is all about my work time. I'm really enjoying everything beyond my office at the moment, and I feel I have enough time for leisure and the family (that's really changed over this past year).

2. Although many of these things cause me great frustration, I've been going through a process of really trying to understand what happens for me around these subjects, and working out fixes. So, although there are still frustrations in there, I either have a plan to fix those things, or I understand where I need to move towards in order to find a fix. So, I need the right help for making some of my projects happen (I need to find the right project manager, designers, etc.), and I need to be able to let go a little in order for them to make things happen.

3. I probably need to switch accountants, too – find someone who speaks English and who is not so complicated. I need to work out what to do with The Hill and just get on and do it. I need to force delegation by limiting even further the number of hours I spend indoors in an office.

4. There's a big overall 'where and how I work' question in there that keeps coming up. And I don't exactly know how to solve this when we move to Fano. One idea I have is to do most of my work from cafés around the town, including cafés on the beach in the summer (I'll need a good computer screen for that). The other idea is to have an office desk that I can stand at, rather than sitting for hours at a time.

What observations and conclusions can *you* make by doing this exercise? Are some ideas coming up for you? You don't have to figure everything out yet, as there's lots more to come in this book. But you might well already have had some pretty illuminating insights into how to change things in your life for the better.

Exercise 3: Going fishing

Right, here are some more questions (in bold) to allow us to further explore what we love doing, and what we'd love to do.

If you could take a year off, what would you do?

I'm going to give you enough money to cover all your costs for the year: let's say 18 months' salary (to give you some funds to play with, too). This Friday is your last day at work. What would you do for the year? (By the way, I'm borrowing this question from my friend John Williams, author of *Screw Work, Let's Play*.)

Really think this through. If you imagine you'd like to spend the year on the beach, or travelling, consider how long you'd really enjoy doing that. Once you get bored, what would you like to do next?

Okay, I'll have a little go at this myself then:

I'd like to take my family on a big tour of North America and Australia. Then we'd spend a week at home. Then we'd get back on a plane and go to China, to taste tea in the mountains, and do Tai Chi in the parks.

Okay, then we'd have to get those boys back to school. I'd spend the next three months writing my favourite fiction idea (no, I'm not telling, you'll have to wait). Followed by a month in the studio (though I may be pushing my allowance here) with Simone, creating a full album. Then I'd get down to making 'F**k It Business' happen.

Who do you look at and say: 'Ah, they live the life'?

I have a mate who appears to live the life of Riley. He doesn't seem to work very much; he lies in a lot; he takes loads of holidays; he's always eating out in cafés and restaurants; he's always off somewhere exciting; he's comfortable enough, money-wise, but really doesn't seem to do much; he doesn't worry about money, and he always seems to land on his feet. When I look at him, I think, *How does he do it?*, and *I could do with some of that.* (For what it's worth, I know that he has exactly the same thoughts about me, but for different reasons.)

Though I might sit here now, having done some of these exercises, thinking that I'm doing pretty well with the balance in my life, I think of that mate and say, 'Okay, I could still free things up some more.' Is there anyone in your life who makes you jealous – or do you realize that you should really make some changes yourself? Write it down.

What's your guilty pleasure?

What is it that you turn to, by default, when you need to relax? What can't you stop doing? Is there any way you could incorporate this thing more into your life? Or even get paid to do it?

Mine is listening to, and watching, comedy. I listen to it on the radio, and I watch it on YouTube. Thinking about it now, I realize that I could use comedy sketches in some of the online teaching I do. It would be great to research – and the participants would love it.

What would you do if you knew you couldn't fail?

This is a good question as it bypasses the big stumbling block that many of us have – fear of failure. My instant response to this question is 'Write an even bigger fiction book.' This would be based on an idea that I had five years ago; it's a big idea, but it's also very controversial. Yes, I'd do that. It can't fail, after all. My next idea is to do the biggest F**k It gig ever – to 10,000 people. There would be mass Qigong, music, and inspiring stories – an evening of madness that could change people's lives.

What would you do if you knew there was no chance of you failing?

Exercise 4: Going deep-sea fishing

Okay, so we are, generally, looking at doing what we love, but now I'd like to expand the brief somewhat to see if we can generate more ideas before we get down to making some changes in our lives, and doing these things. So, ask yourself the following questions and note your answers in your journal (I've given some of mine as examples).

Putting aside any 'Yes, buts', without limits, and with the biggest of 'F**k Its', what would you like to have?

Get dreaming, get writing.

Ooooh, I'd love a Thunderbird 1, and a hideout in a mountain – the side of the mountain would open up and I could zoom out to go and rescue people.

Too much? Okay. I'd get a Henry Moore sculpture for the garden. I'd like that lovely house we saw in Fano, with the garden on the first floor. Weird. I'd like a waterbed. I'd like a Ferrari. And a garage to put it in. No, not a garage – an underground hideaway, kitted out like the Batcave.

Too much? Well, it would be nice to have a butler.

Too much? Okay, I wave a magic wand and get all the top-class help with the business that I need.

Putting aside any 'Yes, buts', without limits, and with the biggest of 'F**k Its', what (or who) would you like to be?

I'd like to be Harrison Ford: the way he was in the early 80s, *Blade Runner* time.

Too much? I'd like to be calm no matter what. I'd like to be present whatever's going on. I'd like to be kind, even when other people aren't. I'd like to be open, even when everything is closing.

Putting aside any 'Yes, buts', without limits, and with the biggest of 'F**k Its', what would you like to do?

I'd like to have fizzy energy beams streaming out of my palms that can heal anyone in pain, fill the loveless with love, make the sad laugh, turn the anxious into chilled-out hippies, and manifest gold coins for the homeless and struggling. Zap zap zap.

Too much? I'd like to go out tonight and give £10 to every homeless person I meet, no exception. I'd like to eat a burger in a diner. I'd like to bring Bob the Buddha, the character in my book of the same name, to the world and make him famous, so Buddha energy is spread round the world, just by people realizing that they don't have to do anything to be fully awake, they just have to… wake up.

I'd like to lie in more in the mornings. I'd like to be in my wife's arms. I'd like to say F**k It on TV. I'd like to ask Paul McCartney about his 'Sod it' moment. I'd like to score a penalty against goalkeeper David De Gea. I'd like to…

Ahhhh, I could go on. But you get the picture. And getting the picture is the point here. So, by now, you should know whether you're generally doing what you love, or not. You should realize why it's a good idea to be doing as much of what you love as you can. And you should now have a good long list of all the things that you love – both now, and from the past, and potential things that you might love in the future. You also have the bogey list – the things in your current life that you really don't enjoy.

How do you know whether you love something or not?

It's a funny question this one: surely we know what we love and what we don't? But it becomes more relevant as we start to do what we love more often. Sometimes we find that something we thought we loved (or did love in the past), we no longer do. Life moves on.

So here's a quick checklist to ascertain if you really do love something:

* Do you look forward to doing this thing?

* Does it make you feel energetic, or tired, when you do it?

* Would you do it for nothing?

* If you didn't have to do it, would you still do it?

* Put aside any embarrassment you might feel if you don't love it any more… do you still love it?

You might also have some clear ideas already, from working with your journal, about how you can do more of what you love. If not, don't worry. We have a lot more time together.

And now it's time to explore more about how to Do What You Love – the chapter that blatantly plagiarizes the title of the book. Do these chapter-heading-namers have no imagination, for goodness' sake?

4

DO WHAT YOU LOVE

*'People are always blaming circumstances
for what they are. I don't believe in
circumstances. The people who get on in
this world are the people who get up and
look for the circumstances they want, and,
if they can't find them, make them.'*

GEORGE BERNARD SHAW, *MRS WARREN'S PROFESSION*

We're now getting to see how we can Do What We Love. How exciting.

However, the 'Yes, buts' – those 'objections' that seem to prevent you from doing what you want to do – have probably started to arise. Although by now you may have a clear idea of some of the things you could be doing to bring yourself more joy – and the paths you could take to get there – you're still getting the 'Yes, buts'.

If we're going to make a success of starting to Do What We Love, we need to answer these 'Yes, buts'. Whether they are around a lack of clarity, or courage, or time, or money or sense of deserving. We'll be doing that soon.

THE 'BIGGEST CHANGE' EXERCISE

But first we're going to do an exercise that will bring up even more 'Yes, buts' before we address them. Go through your journal notes so far – your responses to the questions you asked yourself in the last chapter – and pull out your six favourite 'Do What You Loves' that you're *not* currently doing. Choose the ones that will create the biggest change in your life.

I've just gone through my notes, and these are my six: some are big, others small, but all would create change in my life:

1. Lose the office and work from cafés in Fano for no more than four hours a day, forever.

2. Write that fiction book.

3. Tour around the USA: start in New York and finish by holding hands with Gaia in San Francisco – the place we got engaged.

4. Write two blogs, every single week: one for personal, one for business. Make them famous.

5. Publish my book *Bob the Buddha*; create a Bob Museum in London.

6. Create a brand new F**k It business, aimed at businesses, called 'F**k It Business'.

Now you have your six dream 'Do What You Loves', create no more than three steps that will take you towards making them happen. Here are mine:

1. Lose the office and work from cafés in Fano for no more than four hours a day, forever.

Step 1: Move to Fano this summer.

Step 2: Find a file-storing and meeting solution (one small office for an assistant only? Room in home?).

Step 3: Find a project manager in order to free up more of my time.

2. Write that fiction book.

Step 1: Plan the book in July, while we're away.

Step 2: Book several weeks away to write solidly on the book (as I am now, for this one).

3. Tour around the USA: start in New York and finish by holding hands with Gaia in San Francisco – the place we got engaged.

Step 1: Put aside the time for this in next year's schedule. Do it now (before it gets booked up).

Step 2: Calculate how much it will cost, and budget for it.

Step 3: Book the flights and the first few hotels.

4. Write two blogs, every single week: one for personal, one for business. Make them famous.

Step 1: Register the two new urls.

Step 2: Brief the Wordpress templates, with relevant headers, to designer.

Step 3: Choose one morning a week to write, and stick to it.

5. Publish **Bob the Buddha;** *create a Bob Museum in London.*

Step 1: Create a hard copy mock-up of the book.

Step 2: Meet with Hay House to share ideas about publishing the book.

Step 3: When publishing date is known, start to plan the 'Museum'.

*6. Create a brand new F**k It business, aimed at businesses, called 'F**k It Business'.*

Step 1: Book a two-day event in London, subject unknown, for one year ahead.

Step 2: Send an email to our mailing list, asking people what 'F**k It Business' could mean for them.

Step 3: Create three online course product ideas based on what people want.

Wow, this is feeling good. Can you see how it works when you start to get down to the detail? Clearly you can go into much more detail if you want. You could do a mind-map for each topic too – where you'd note down ALL the steps you'd need to take, divided into sub-areas. You can also put precise dates to everything when you're ready.

Tackling the 'Yes, buts'

Yes, but… Have your 'Yes, buts' started coming up?

On your six favourite 'Do What You Loves' you may have a 'Yes, but' for the topic itself (for example, 'I just don't have the time') and you may also have a 'Yes, but' for each of its steps. Just look at your list and steps again and, even if they haven't come up naturally, start to write down some 'Yes, buts'.

Here's an example: I won't go through all the steps for each topic, but I'll note down my 'Yes, buts' around that broad topic.

1. Lose the office and work from cafés in Fano for no more than four hours a day, forever.

Yes, but what about when I need a bigger screen? Or when I need to be on my own? Or when I need to do a private Skype meeting? Or when I need to work with a few files or books (as I do now)?

2. Write that fiction book.

Yes, but that's a real indulgence. I've got things that I really like doing that can earn money for the family, so why waste time on a project like this, which is unlikely to earn any cash?

3. Tour around the USA: start in New York and finish by holding hands with Gaia in San Francisco – the place we got engaged.

Yes, but that's going to cost a fortune. Isn't it best to wait until the year after next? We shouldn't burn money that we might need for something more important.

4. Write two blogs, every single week, one for personal, one for business. Make them famous.

Yes, but I'll put in all the effort and no one will read them – how on earth do you get new people to read a blog anyway, when there are so many thousands out there?

*5. Publish **Bob the Buddha**; create a Bob Museum in London.*

Yes, but… errmmmm…. No, buts… Just need to do this. It's a relatively easy win (I've written the book already) and it will be brilliant to see it out there in the world.

6. *Create a brand new F**k It business, aimed at businesses, called 'F**k It Business'.*

Yes, but the people who know F**k It just for its therapeutic message might react to the corporate-capitalist nature of this one.

And then, clearly, you could go through and answer those 'Yes, buts'. Just to show you how, I'll look at the last one:

6. *Create a brand new F**k It business, aimed at businesses, called 'F**k It Business'.*

Yes, but the people who know F**k It just for its therapeutic message might react to the corporate-capitalist nature of this one.

The F**k It credit card: for people who say, 'F**k It, I'll buy that'.

Answer: Well, don't force it on anyone. Offer it only as a sign-up option to our mailing list, or to anyone for that matter. Something along the lines of: 'If you'd like to know how F**k It could work for your business, sign up here.' Then we can send messages (and blog links) *only* to those who've opted in. Job done.

Incidentally, understanding the 'Yes, buts' – otherwise known as 'objections' to anything you do – when we're talking about a business offer, for example, is business gold.

Let's see… I'll take some random words from those last few sentences (a random technique such as this can be a great way to create brand spanking new ideas) – 'sign', 'gold', F**k It. Okay, so we'll create a F**k It credit card: one that people can use to say 'F**k It, I'll buy that.'

Great idea, Parkin. Objections, anyone?

How can I trust you? – you're not a financial institution.

Well, we wouldn't be able to set this up without a financial institution. So the organization that we partner with to do this has to be well-known enough to be recognized by everyone out there. I think HSBC runs a credit card partnership scheme, for example.

It's highly irresponsible to suggest that people should say F**k It and buy stuff on credit. It could put people into debt, with all the misery that brings.

Yes, good point. Maybe, then, this is a 'F**k It, treat yourself' card: that's a credit card you have to *charge* with a monthly amount of your choosing. It would be like saving – you'd drop £100 a month onto your treat card, then go out and use it when you fancy treating yourself. That would be a responsible way of treating yourself, and it'd make the card very different to other cards (our objection to this would be that it might be much harder to do).

That's just another way to make money from us, isn't it? I thought you wanted to help people.

Good you asked that, because in fact, 20 per cent of our profits go to the 'F**k It Foundation', which offers 'Escape Funding' for those stuck in jobs they hate, so they can pursue their dream of doing what they love; it supports them with a six-month financial 'cushion' to get their new venture going.

So, do you see how understanding, and responding to, objections can create really interesting new ideas? It will probably be the same for you, as you look at your 'Yes, buts'.

F**K IT, I CAN DO WHAT I LOVE.

*This F**k It Push Mantra: If you're prone to guilt,
if you're selfless to the point of exhaustion, if you
always join the back of the queue, if you always
say, 'No, please: you go first' — this one's for you.*

Now we're going to be looking at some responses to the significant
'Yes, buts' — such as how can we find the time, or the money, to Do
What We Love? But first, we're going to sit down together and talk
about 'purpose': the 'why' behind the thing you'd love to do.

FINDING THE PURPOSE

*'Decide upon your major definite purpose in life
and then organize all your activities around it.'*
BRIAN TRACY — AUTHOR AND MOTIVATIONAL SPEAKER.

Yes, pour yourself a glass of whisky, or whatever's your tipple of
choice, and come sit with me in these armchairs next to this roaring
fire. There's a storm raging outside, but we're safe in here.

It's time to have a discussion. About purpose. Because just about
any book you pull from the self-help shelves will, early on, insist that
finding your purpose in life is a critical step. Once you've found that
purpose, then everything starts to work, as you're focused and the
whole universe conspires to help you achieve it.

Here are some life purpose statements that I found during a quick
search on the web; I'll tell you their authors in a minute:

'To uplift humanity's consciousness through business.'

'To leave the world a better place than I found it – for horses and for people, too.'

'To humbly serve the Lord by being a loving, playful, powerful and passionate example of the absolute joy that's available to us the moment we rejoice in God's gifts and sincerely love and serve all his creations.'

What do you think of these statements? (This is us, remember, by the fire, having a discussion).

Do you want to have a go at noting down *your* life purpose before we move on? Because your overall purpose could be the 'why?' that gives all the things you (love to) do direction. Go on, just scribble it down on the back of an envelope. It doesn't have to take long: that one-sentence summary of the purpose of the whole of your life.

Sorry, was I sounding a bit sarcastic there? You're probably starting to sniff my take on this. Believe me, if I could locate my life purpose and note it down in one handy sentence that I could then tattoo on the back of my hand so I was always and forever 'on purpose', I would. I've tried (not the tattooing bit, but the purpose summation bit). I really have. Several times.

And it's more than the fact that it brings out the slightly indecisive side of me: 'Ooohh, should I use the word "creative" or "playful"? Which one best sums up what I do? It's so important.' A lot more. Again, have a go and see how you get on.

> **If I could locate my life purpose and turn it into a tattoo, I would.**

It's also that it only reflects one side of us, usually a projected 'best' side. Take the statement, from 'D.C. Cordova, co-founder of the Excellerated Business School': *'To uplift humanity's consciousness through business.'*

I mean, where do you start? First off, here's someone who probably enjoys the large parts of business that have nothing to do with 'uplifting humanity's consciousness' — the big meetings, the swanky dos, the thrill of success, the dollars in the bank and the flash cars, the respect, and so on.

And what does it mean — to 'uplift humanity's consciousness'? How do you track that? Well, the latest Humanity Consciousness figures have come through, and they're up: great news! And how would you know whether you'd had anything to do with it? Eight out of 10 members of humanity whose consciousness had been uplifted over the last year said it was down to D.C. Cordova and her consciousness-uplifting business activities.

Now I don't know D.C. Cordova, or anything about her (I'm intentionally not researching her; all I know is that she's a she not a he), but I wonder what her intention for herself and her business would be if she were completely honest? Maybe it would be more like: *'Be really successful with my business by helping others be successful, and enjoy to the full all the fruits of this success, including having a beach house in Malibu that I drive to in my Porsche.'*

And what about: *'To leave the world a better place than I found it — for horses and for people, too.'* That's from one Monty Roberts, author of *The Man Who Listens to Horses.* Where do you start with that one? Let's leave aside the horses and people bit for a second, and just stick with *'To leave the world a better place than I found it'.*

So, and this is not an exhaustive list:

* How are we judging this? What makes the world a 'better' or 'worse' place when you leave it compared to when you found it? Levels of poverty? Number of cars per family?

Average global happiness levels? The number of people killed in wars that year? The number of toffee apples produced per year?

* Even if we could find a metric for judgement, what effect are you likely to have had on the world in order to make it 'better'? Seriously? I mean, who are you, Jesus?

* What are the consequences if you fail in this purpose (though, granted, you're only judged once you've left this world)? Has your life been completely futile?

So now let's look at the 'for horses and for people, too' bit. Well, I suppose it does define the metric somewhat, though I don't know how we'd ever judge whether the world was a better place for horses. Even if we took one state of the USA, how are we going to know whether anything is 'better' for the horses there? Do they like to gambol over the plains, wild and free? Or do they prefer to be mollycoddled and groomed, petted and adored by humans? Ah, maybe this guy does know, as he can 'listen to horses'.

And I LOVE the fact that 'people' are an add-on, 'too'. Like a throwaway, 'After I've cleaned the kitchen, I'll quickly dust the dining room.' It's 'Once I've improved the welfare of all the horses on the planet, I'll then turn my attention to the humans.' I think there's some kind of God complex going on there: 'To bring peace to the world, to end all wars and suffering, and to give horses their true voice.'

Maybe purpose is (naturally) your thing

This isn't to say that you can't have a huge sense of purpose — and a huge purpose — and have a huge effect in the world. Just look at what these hugely purposeful people (who I've plucked randomly from my head) achieved: Gandhi, Alexander Fleming (who discovered penicillin), Winston Churchill, Henry Ford, Thomas Edison, JFK, Jeremy Clarkson… and, oh God, there's the dark side of purpose, too: just look at Hitler and Stalin.

And maybe the big purpose thing IS your thing (and I'm talking about positive stuff here). Maybe you've known it for a long time. Maybe it's what drives you every day. Maybe you have no real choice – it's just something you have to do. Maybe you love doing it too, in which case, lucky you: what are you doing reading this? You're on track, you're loving what you do, and I bet things are really working for you, aren't they?

Say F**k It to the idea of having one big purpose.

Yes, lucky you. But what about the rest of us? We, the masses, who –

1. Don't seem to have been handed (or discovered for ourselves) an irresistible mission on this planet.

2. Even when we have a mission, and are into it, we then move on to something else.

3. Are motivated by such a variety of opposing forces and desires: to help others, but also, at times, to put ourselves first; to do good, but also to be a little wicked too.

For us, putting our life's 'purpose' into a sentence is either inaccurate or temporary, or just plain limiting.

F**K IT, I DON'T NEED THIS.

*This F**k It Push Mantra: Imagine holding out
your hand when you say this one – in the way a
child does when they say 'no' to something.*

Oh, but John, you might say (and people do), your purpose is clear – after all you've helped hundreds of thousands of people, in one way or another, with your down-to-earth and humorous advice and philosophy. That's your gift… that's your purpose, surely?

But I don't see it like that. Even with this one book as an example: my purpose is, yes, to help loads of people find what they love and do it. I mean it should be, like, AMAZING, for me that this collection of pages can go out there and actually help people be happier in what they do, every day.

But I have to write that in order to *feel* it a little. I do feel it when I get the emails from people, thanking me, but it's not my entire 'purpose'. I'm not writing this book just for you (sorry). I'm writing it because… (now let me try to be as honest as I can here) –

* I want to remind myself how to keep on track, and keep doing what I love.

* 'Doing what I love' is an ongoing mission for me. I've discovered some great ideas around it, and I just want to share them with you, like mates.

* This writing process with a deadline squeezes interesting stuff – some useful stuff, some funny stuff – out of my head in a very unique way, and I like that. The creative process

in itself is satisfying; sure, it's frustrating at times, but it's satisfying... I get into that 'flow' thing we were talking about earlier, where time disappears and I'm completely absorbed.

* I like 'producing' something that goes out there with my name on it. I like walking into a bookshop and seeing my books there. Not because of the effect the books might be having, but just because it makes me feel proud of myself.

* The books are successful – this is an ego-thing again, but F**k It, I like doing well; I like it that people like my stuff. Please feel free to come over and pat me and tell me how brilliant I am. We all want that, don't we? It's just hard to admit to it.

* It's a pretty good way to earn cash for living, paying the mortgage, buying clothes for the boys and taking the family on holiday. That I write this book and then the cash continues to arrive for years is a bonus, and a bonus that's very relevant to this book.

* Writing stuff like this is on my list – when I do it – of Doing What I Love: it's what I've loved doing in the past, it's what I love doing in the present (in this moment) and I suspect doing some version of this is what I'll love doing in the future. Sure, it's not all pure joy. In fact, it can be pretty darned tough at times: working out how best to convey a point, finding the right rhythm and the right words and the right tone... it has its tension, but I like that too, actually, if truth be told. It seems that the tension, the 'squeezing' I just referred to, is necessary to the product.

That's me being honest – I do this for a whole range of reasons.

We do F**k It in general for a whole range of reasons too. Sure, it's lovely that it helps people, but I don't do it just for that. Maybe I could sum up the range of reasons in one (longish) sentence. Anthony Robbins (you know him, don't you?) did that in his:

> *'To humbly serve the Lord by being a loving, playful, powerful and passionate example of the absolute joy that's available to us the moment we rejoice in God's gifts and sincerely love and serve all his creations.'*

Though mine clearly wouldn't read like that. Mine would have words like 'irreverently', 'creatively' and 'provocatively'. But it would still be a fixed and probably limited and temporary reflection of something I am (and I suspect you are too): a moving, changing, flowing, mixed-up, inconsistent, variably motivated, selfless and selfish, good and bad, brilliant and rubbish, entertaining and boring kind of person.

For me, that's what a person is – a vessel for life energy to come flowing through. And if I put the message out to the universe that this vessel is only open to this kind of energy, then, sure, I'll probably get good at channelling that kind of energy, but it blocks me as a vessel for all the other life energies.

We do Fk It for a whole range of reasons.**

It seems to me that the problem for most of us is that we have placed lots of tags on ourselves (and had them placed on us by others); we have limited ourselves through our beliefs (about ourselves and the world) and shut ourselves down through our perceived obligations… so that we haven't been open vessels for that life energy. And having a fixed purpose can so easily add to that tagging ('I'm *this* kind of person, me – with this kind of purpose, and nothing else.')

My invitation (to you, and me) is to open, not close.

Following the compulsion

I've identified something in my life that allows me to do what I love, and follow my flow, and it may well help you too. It can easily be misinterpreted, but it sums up what I feel most accurately – COMPULSION.

'Compulsion' is a very F**k It drive.

This is not the compulsion to do certain things that is placed on us by others, but the compulsion we feel just to do something. It's stronger than that word 'flow', or even 'desire'. There's an element of force about it. This morning, I should have been looking at a dozen urgent emails, but I felt the COMPULSION just to get writing about this 'purpose' thing. So I didn't resist it. 'Compulsion' is very F**k It: 'F**k It, I just have to do this.'

I see that many of the most interesting things I've done have been inspired by this sense of compulsion – I simply *had* to do them. If I'd had a fixed purpose, I might have discarded certain compulsions because they didn't fit with that purpose. However, if I follow my compulsion, that becomes my purpose. The rest happens naturally.

If you're starting to feel a compulsion to Do What You Love in your life – I've used the singular there, but I refer to the plural: not just one thing you love, but the ever-changing things that you love – then that compulsion (desire on steroids, if you will) can be your purpose in itself.

F**K IT, I MUST DO IT.

This F**k It Push Mantra: When the compulsion takes you, use this mantra to follow through.

And now I feel compelled to talk about courage. Fancy another whisky? My, that was a good chat we had, wasn't it?

FINDING THE COURAGE

'Life is an ongoing process of choosing between safety (out of fear and need for defense) and risk (for the sake of progress and growth). Make the growth choice a dozen times a day.'
ABRAHAM MASLOW, US PSYCHOLOGIST

I dig Abe's observation here. I'm just struggling with the frequency thing: 'a dozen times a day'? That's what, four or five times before lunch? Do I really have to make four or five such choices before lunchtime? I can't see it: my main choices at that time of day are whether to have eggs or yoghurt for breakfast, or to drink rooibos or yogi tea. Yes, really.

'Whatever you can do, or dream you can do, begin it.
Boldness has genius, power, and magic in it. Begin it now.'
JOHANN WOLFGANG VON GOETHE

Aha, now this I like. Very inspiring, that Goethe. A way with words, ahem, okay – 'Der Worte sind genug gewechselt, lasst mich auch endlich Taten sehn!' A way with words, you see.

(At least, that's what I wanted to say: I imagined this famous Goethe quote must be a direct translation from the original German. But it isn't, and it's a real stretch to suggest it's a loose translation of a line from *Faust* I've used there. Funny I should make that point, really, that Goethe had a way with words, because these certainly aren't his English words, and they are pretty certainly not translated from his original German words, and therefore they are probably nothing to do with his words at all.)

If you've realized what it is that you love doing, but know you don't do it enough (and that, by the way, is an appropriate place to be at this stage in the book) — even if you're increasingly feeling the 'compulsion' to do it — there are a few possible reasons why you're not doing it, and because of these you'll struggle to do it.

And the first reason is f… f… f… f… fear.

Fear of failure. Fear of embarrassment. Fear of exposure. Fear of change. Fear of loss. Fear of peeing your pants. Yes, really. Good story alert. Coming soon.

Have a look now at what you'd love to be doing, and see if you can spot the things that would 'scare' in there, if you started to do them. It may not be the things themselves; it may be more the reaction of those around you. Maybe the thought of paragliding down Everest doesn't scare you, but it will freak out your family. So you're afraid of how they'll deal with it. But usually the fear is around failing, or embarrassing ourselves.

❝❝❝❝❝❝❝❝❝❝❝❝❝❝❝❝❝❝❝❝❝❝❝❝❝

I said F**k It and quit my job to become a self-employed journalist and writer. It kinda happened by itself because I was open to the idea and didn't listen to my fears (or other people's fears, for that matter).

It felt right and even though it still feels scary sometimes, it still feels right. I loved what I did, but I didn't love the place where I did it, so now I am writing in my own space, travelling the world and working towards a location-independent office.

ANNE VAN DEN BERG, ZWOLLE – THE NETHERLANDS

❞❞❞❞❞❞❞❞❞❞❞❞❞❞❞❞❞❞❞❞❞❞❞❞❞❞

Okay, okay, I'll tell you that story now, as it does constitute a nice F**k It parable. (I think that's the first time the word 'parable' has been used near the phrase F**k It: I should do that more often.)

Finding the courage to make music

So you know by now that, over the past few years, making music has been one of the key areas in which I've been doing what I love. Having realized that I wanted to start making music again (as a kid and a teenager, I'd tinkered around on the piano and guitar), I began trying to create it digitally.

*That's the first time 'parable' and 'F**k It' have been used together.*

But I've had to confront my fears at every stage. I struggled to work out how to use the technology to make the music (the software 'Ableton Live'); once I understood the technology, I struggled to get what was in my head working. I struggled to make elaborate musical parts work together, and I struggled to make my voice work.

So it did scare me, and there were many times when I considered giving up (you can ask Gaia). Even at the first stage – getting the software to work on my computer – I struggled for months to make it work. I was frustrated, and I was scared: scared of failing, scared of being rubbish, scared I'd make a fool of myself by investing so much time in something that was ultimately no good.

But I had this compulsion to make the music. The thought that I could, one day, create the kind of tunes that I love listening to myself, and playing them to an audience – to have other people dancing to the electronic music I'd made – kept me at it. The compulsion to create, and follow it through to some form of ultimate creation (a whole gig?), was very strong. And so I did keep going.

F**K IT, I CAN DO IT.

*This F**k It Push Mantra: If you're really stretching
yourself, and sometimes want to give up – or you
lose hope that you'll ever succeed – remember
that with a good F**k It, you can do it.*

I did do a gig actually, in the autumn of 2013: it was a two-hour
'F**k It Experience' for 300 people at Bush Hall in London. It was
one mother of a scary experience. But I want to describe another
particular experience that had a very particular manifestation of fear,
and that happened more than a year before the gig.

By the spring of 2012, I'd really started to create some interesting
music. I had one track in particular, *Say F**k It and Be Free*, that was
working. My publisher, Hay House, had asked me to do a 20-minute
talk at their 'I Can Do It' weekend in London, and as part of that, I
decided to perform, in front of 1,000 people, *Say F**k It and Be Free*
(prior to this event, I'd not played my music to more than 10 people
at a time).

In fact, I used the song, and the performance of it, to talk about
how we can, if we want to, say F**k It, do what we love, and do
some extraordinary things. And those 20 minutes really were
extraordinary. The audience really got on my side: they understood
what a big thing this was for me, and how courageous I was to
perform my music for the first time in front of so many people.
When I played the song, everyone got up on their feet: dancing,
clapping, joining in with the chorus.

It was AMAZING, a total blast. And the experience of just those
few minutes on stage made all the struggles and the challenges

worthwhile. I had done what I loved. I was doing what I loved. I'd had the balls to get up on stage and do it. And that's the fabulous feeling you get when you Do What You Love.

But on that day, no one was aware of what I'd gone through just before I went on stage. I saved that story for the year after, when I returned to 'I Can Do It' for another 20-minute slot. I know exactly what I said during those 20 minutes because I scripted the talk very carefully; I learned it word for word, with the right actions at the right time. And, by just accessing the file now on my computer I can reproduce here the story I told on that day:

Script for 'I Can Do It', 2013

So, if you were here this time last year you'll remember that I stood up here and did something for the first time… I played some of the music I'd created and recorded. And because I was doing that, I was nervous.

What I didn't tell you is what had happened in the minutes before I came on. Now, what I'm about to say is very embarrassing for me. And as a consequence, it's probably very funny for you. It's a risk for me to tell you this, but F**k It, let's go.

It was 10 minutes before I was due on stage, and I thought I'd better go for one last pee. I don't know about you, but I try to pace my pees. People do this before they travel: they tend to 'get one in' for the road. I didn't want to get caught out mid-talk, so I thought I'd have one last pee.

So I'm in a cubicle, doing my thing, and calming myself down for my talk. I zip up, and I turn round to open the door and leave. At that point, I happen to look down and I see… well, let's say I see a liquid stain on my light-coloured trousers.

Somehow, for a moment, I had missed… and hit the leg of my trousers. Now that may not be a surprising fact to many of you women out there – that a man could 'miss' – but it was surprising and disturbing for me in that moment. I felt the world falling away from me. I looked away, and then looked back. It was still there. I thought I was going to have a heart attack. Literally. I looked at my watch. I had eight minutes left 'til I would be up in front of 1,000 people.

I had to act. I burst out of the cubicle, and looked for a hand dryer. There wasn't one. I pulled at a tissue, and started wiping frantically at the stain, but it only left moist little bits of paper. And the stain got slightly bigger.

Seven minutes to go. I had to find another loo.

I went out of the backstage area and into the public area, which was FULL of people, as it was a break in the programme. Trying to hold my water bottle over my stain, I hobbled across to the public loos. In there, thank the Lord, were two beautiful, shining, stainless-steel hand dryers. YES.

I wanted to kiss them but thought that probably wasn't a great idea, hygiene-wise. I relaxed. I went over to one of the dryers and waved my hand underneath it, then lifted up my leg to allow the warm stream of air to blast away my embarrassment. But within seconds, the warm air cut out. I waved my hand again, but nothing happened.

Lots more waving, lots more nothing. So I hopped – yes, hopped – over to the next dryer, and that wouldn't even start. I was now standing on one leg, waving both arms under the dryers, in desperation.

And at this point I want to press pause, and examine my thought process. My thought process – with six minutes to go until I'd be in front of 1,000 people, with an obvious pee stain on my trouser leg – was this:

Okay, okay, think, John. Right, the only option is to say F**k It and go right ahead onto the stage with your head held high. Who cares, after all? And I cringed at the thought. *I* cared. *People* would care. I couldn't do that.

Plan B. I should say F**k It and just run away. I would just leave the building by the front entrance, hail a taxi, then get on a plane and go home, back to Italy. And cry for a while. Sure, I'd probably never be invited back. Or maybe never invited anywhere again. But I'd save my embarrassment, at least.

Noooo, I couldn't do that either. I needed Plan T. Yes, it was time for Plan T. I needed to say 'F**k It, I can't work this one out. I can't find a solution. I just need to Trust (*that's the T by the way*), and take one step after another.'

And so I did. Five minutes to go. I relaxed. I took one step after another and returned to the backstage area. There, I got into a conversation with the lovely Robert Holden. I got so lost in this conversation that it kind of surprised me when, a few minutes later, I was called to go up on stage.

And as I started doing my talk in front of all those people, I remembered something. I looked down and there was nothing on my trousers. All was dry. I thanked the gods, and I thanked Robert Holden – did he have magic powers of pee-stain evaporation?

And I thanked this beautiful phrase, F**k It, for helping me to let go and Trust in that moment of need.

There: not only was I willing to tell this story to at least another 1,000 people, I've also told it here, where many (many) more people will read it. But I want you to see that doing what you love is rarely plain sailing. Getting out there and doing something – being willing to fail, and being willing to embarrass yourself – takes a lot of guts.

And I'll tell you something else too – something that will hopefully inspire you to get out there and do it, and to overcome the inevitable challenges you'll face along the way. You might

With one big F**k It, You Can Do It Too.

be thinking, *Oh well, John is confident and sure of himself, so of course he can do these things in the end – even if there are some hiccups along the way,* but in fact, I was a very shy boy, and teenager. I was horrified at the idea of getting up and talking in front of other people, and for many years I just wanted to hide and do my own thing.

The thought of voluntarily putting myself on stage in front of others and performing a song would have had me soiling myself, not just peeing myself. But I grew up. And I faced those fears; I faced down my instinct to run away and hide. I had (and still have) things to say, and I wanted to say them to a lot of people. So there I was. And here I am. Doing what I love, even though it's not always easy. And that means you can do it too. With an 'I Can Do It' and one big 'F**k It', You Can Do It Too.

"""""""""""""""""""""""""""""

I said F**k It to the fear that was holding me back. I now have a lovely partner, two gorgeous girls and a wonderful fat cat. A little further along my journey, I took my hands off the steering wheel (said F**k It again) and gave up my corporate job. I now work for myself and have a lovely work-life balance – happy days!

PIPPA OLD – BUCKINGHAMSHIRE, UK

,,,,,,,,,,,,,,,,,,,,,,,,,,,,,,,,

FINDING THE MOMENT

All things in the universe conspire to enable you to do just what's right for you and everybody else, at just the right time, without exception. So there's always the perfect moment to do whatever it is you love…

Believing that there's a 'right moment' to do something is one of the top three excuses for not getting on and doing it *now*. So it's kind of best to ignore that first paragraph, and concentrate on this one instead:

The moment is now. Get on and do it. Say F**k It and make your move. Drop everything and get started: start to play, start to build, start to plan, start to write, start to sell, start to sing, start to research, start to paint, start to promise, start to cook, start to make a few pennies… by doing what you love.

F**K IT, IT'S NOW OR NEVER.

*This F**k It Push Mantra: Sometimes it's true, sometimes it's not. But this mantra will give you the required push when you need it.*

FINDING THE TIME

Of course you don't have the time. No one has the time these days. I don't. You don't. No one does. But it wasn't always like this.

Not so long ago, we all had more time. We used to sit around and talk and twiddle our thumbs. We used to wonder what to do, and then play cards. We'd flick between the three channels on the TV, then turn it off and be... bored. Yes, bored. Being bored is what happens when you have lots of time and nothing to do with it.

Back in the day there would be whole crowds of people just wandering the streets, and through the countryside, just bored. Like gangs, but without the impulse to do anything. Because there was nothing to do. Today, 'bored' is becoming such a rare state to be in that the folks at the *Oxford English Dictionary* are considering taking the word out of the next edition. There's just so little use for it nowadays. But they are so busy with all the new words that are coming in, they haven't the time to take out the old ones.

People used to have the time, yes. In fact, they'd have so much time, and so little to do with it, they'd dream up stupid ways to kill time: such as killing each other. In the past there were more wars because there was less to do. It was a way of keeping yourself, and your millions of restless young people, busy. Soon, very few people had the problem of what to do with their time: because they had none.

* Maybe a secret aim of the United Nations (UN), after the last big one, was to try to keep everyone busy, so they wouldn't go around killing each other for something to do. Maybe the UN is responsible for the astonishing proliferation of Things to Do.

* Maybe the UN masterminded the virus-like email systems that hang over our lives.

* Maybe they secretly fund the vast amount of pointless but diverting television programming, the gossip magazines, the mindless video games, the unappealing apps. Maybe they've secretly fed the media with a whole range of Things to Do ideas: 1,000 Things to Do Before You Die; Be an Expert This and an Expert That.

* Maybe the UN have rigged the housing markets around the world, so having a decent roof over your head means you have to work ever harder to earn ever more money, just to pay off the loan on that roof.

So we used to have the time, but now we don't. So what to do about it? You've got this thing that you love, or suspect that you *would* love, and you'd like to spend some time doing it, but you just don't have any time. Your days are filled by doing things that you just about tolerate – whether it's a job that you just about get through, or the chores outside work that you just about manage. It's enough just to get yourself through to having some mindless time in front of the TV.

F**K IT, NO MORE EXCUSES.

*This F**k It Push Mantra: Ooohhh, we're so good at excuses. I could write a book about the excuses I have for not doing this or that (and for doing this or that). And it would be very easy to write. But excuses are boring. Cleanse them from your life with this mantra.*

Because this is a leading (and genuine) reason for not doing what we love. If we can crack it, we get to open a significant door to being able to do more of what we love. Helmets on, let's go:

Prioritize doing what you love

It sounds so obvious. It *is* so obvious. But that word 'prioritize' is so tame and overused that we ride past it in our attempt to sort things out. But prioritizing can be a bloody and ruthless business. It's why real prioritizing needs to be laced with frequent 'F**k Its'.

For example, I do not have time to write this book. I really don't. And that's because I prioritize a lot of the non-work things in my life. I always have my lunch and dinner sitting down with my family. I always have a daily walk (I sound like a dog: I'm fed and walked). I always have a nap in the afternoon (now I sound like a cat). So, what with getting the boys off to school, picking them up, preparing and clearing up meals, ferrying the boys around, the eating and sleeping and walking… it doesn't leave so much time for work.

> *Real prioritizing needs to be laced with frequent 'F**k Its'.*

Well it leaves, at the most, five or six hours a day for work, actually. And five or six hours is just about the right amount of time to stay just below 'on top of everything' – which is where I like to be. Being on top of everything makes me flabby. Stretching a bit keeps me hungry and efficient. Oh, and I've not mentioned the holidays and weekends away – we have lots of those.

So I really don't have time to write this book. Just like you don't have time to Do What You Love (and maybe, for you too, that's writing a book). So, how did this book get written and thus into your eyeline?

Not by some delicate process of 'prioritizing'. It's not among the nine things that I have to do. It's not neatly shuffled into its place on the priority list and ticked off with the rest of them.

Introducing Priority Bully

No, this book got written by being a bully. By throwing its weight around. By standing in front of all the other things on my priority list, looking them in the eye, and then punching them hard on the nose. This book got written by saying, 'This Thursday, I'm writing.' I try to clear other stuff – I try to finish important things on my to-do list – but it never happens. Other things don't stand aside so easily, so they have to be smacked on the nose, or simply ignored.

It's not been easy. The mentality of ignoring everything else – of putting everything else outside our head whilst we get on and do something – is different to the multi-tasking managing-director side of our brain.

Now I sit here, 1,000 miles away from my office and home. I have my email on auto-reply for a week. I've delayed things and ignored things. I will have to do that all week. I'm here in a bunker to do one thing only – to write this book. If there's a customer service problem, someone else will have to handle it. If someone is shouting for my attention, they will have to go hoarse.

Because the Priority Bully is in town. I *have* to do this: the compulsion is there. Sure, a deadline is looming, but I also do this with projects that don't have an external deadline. In fact, I create my own deadlines that I treat as seriously as publisher deadlines.

You can do the same. I'm going to be discussing many other ways of organizing your priorities and time so you can do more of what you love, but the Priority Bully is by far the most effective. It is F**k It in action in your temporal backyard. He (or she) stands there, and when approached by another priority or demand, simply says F**k It, and smacks them on the nose. The Priority Bully is the way that you'll be able to spend time doing what you love – no matter how busy you are or think you are. You *will* find the time. You *must*.

Which reminds me of a nice quote by Anthony Robbins: 'If you think you can't, then you must. When you think you must, you can.' And he's a big, strong man. He'd make a good bully model, standing in your temporal backyard.

> *Haven't got the time? F**k It, wham, bam, thank you, ma'am.*

(And, just before I move on to the next point, I'll share with you a discussion that's just gone on in my mental backyard. A little voice in there just said, *John, we're hungry – can we go out and grab some lunch, please?* and the Priority Bully said, *No, fuck off.* So now I'm sitting here eating Weetabix for lunch, which is the only thing I have here. That's Priority Bully in action.)

Do less of what you don't love

Yeah, thanks for that, John. Like I hadn't thought of it. But how? I know – you're doing tons of stuff that you don't love, or positively hate, because you have to. You don't have a choice. It's your job. Or you're doing something for your family. In one way or another, you're obliged to do it. Well, there *are* ways, depending on your resources and your mentality. Some take resources, some take mentality – some take both. Here are a few:

Go part-time or work less

When I was last in a paid job (back in the 1990s, when I was a creative in an advertising agency), I wanted to spend more time doing what I loved (which was screenwriting). Looking back now, given that Gaia and I didn't yet have kids, I can't see why I didn't just carve out the time, but anyway… I asked the agency if I could do a four-day week, and they said 'yes'.

I was the first man at the agency to go part-time, and no one could understand how I'd managed to pull it off. But I just asked. And it worked – for me because I now had one clear day a week to write (as I explained above, you need clear days to write; it's hard to do it in bits. Maybe that answers my own question just now, about carving out the time), and for my employer because I was doing the same amount of work in four days as I'd previously been doing over five.

In fact, here's a message to all employers: I saw that those of us at the agency who worked part-time would get in early and stay late, and work really hard in between to get through what needed to be done in the 20 per cent fewer days that we had. We'd all do (at least) five days' work over four days.

So, when people come to me and say, *Well, I'd love to do this, but there's no way I can give up the job, because blah, blah*, the first thing I ask them is whether they can go part-time. If your 'Yes, but' on this point is not the potential reaction of your employer, but your financial state, then work it out.

It's usually possible to shave 20 per cent or so off your expenses. Eat fewer ready meals from posh supermarkets and more Weetabix with milk, just like me. We managed to slash our spending by a third last year – 'Eat up your Weetabix, boys. No, you can't have any Melanzane alla Parmigiana (Italian aubergine [eggplant] bake with tomato sauce, mozzarella and Parmesan cheese).

Even the UK government have done it (I'm writing this days after the remarkable result of the 2015 UK election, when the spendthrift Tories got back into power with a majority). They've done it with a plan remarkably similar to my own: they insist that vast swathes of the British population eat Weetabix (no milk: milk is for sissies – choke on it if you will, it's good exercise for your lungs!).

And if you are among those who can't afford even a packet of Weetabix (in fact, I'm just looking at my packet and see it's actually a supermarket own-brand version, not 'Weetabix' at all, but 'wholewheat biscuits'), go to one of those food banks. They say this to the masses, of course, between mouthfuls of exquisite Melanzane alla Parmigiana.

But if you can't go part-time (or don't want to), then try to work less. That might mean working more efficiently, and faster, to get the same amount of work done in less time (advice on how to do that coming up). But it might also mean giving up a position or an ambition.

❝❝❝❝❝❝❝❝❝❝❝❝❝❝❝❝❝❝❝❝❝❝❝❝

I said F**k It to having a big apartment and more money and now only work part-time. I now have more time for the things I love, and for building a life that really suits who I am.
EVA-MARIA MAYWALD – MUNICH, GERMANY

❞❞❞❞❞❞❞❞❞❞❞❞❞❞❞❞❞❞❞❞❞❞❞❞

A lawyer from Edinburgh, Scotland, once told me about his journey to 'working less'. He was a partner in a law firm, and was working long hours. He became exhausted and realized he needed to get his life more in balance. So he developed interests out of work, spent more time with his family, and started leaving work at 6 p.m., as the non-partner employees did. As a result, he felt better. He took work less seriously. He no longer put in 110 per cent: it was more like 90 per cent. Well, the other (workaholic) partners noticed this, of course, and they called him in for a chat. They told him they'd seen he was working less, and seemed less committed – to them, 'committed' meant putting in the (endless) hours. He said that he was much happier and felt much more balanced; they said they didn't think this was the way a man with his 'responsibilities' should behave.

> *F**k It, who cares about position, status, salary and a big desk?*

So he offered to give up his responsibilities: or, rather, to step down from being a partner, take a pay cut, and do a very similar job but in the hours (and the style) that he preferred. And the other partners agreed. It was win-win, and he continues to be very happy in that lower-paying but less-taxing job.

If you want to do more of what you love, F**k It, who cares about the position, and the status, and the big desk and the accompanying salary? Buy freedom with money. It's usually possible. How much are you willing to spend on Doing What You Love?

So, if you can, work less. Take your lunch break for once. Go to a gallery (you love art). Start researching that neat business idea you have. Leave on time. Sure, there are more people on the trains and roads then, but you get to dream and plan how you're going to spend your extra time doing what you love.

Shit, looking at that packet of supermarket own-brand wholewheat biscuits, I reckon I've eaten seven of them while writing that last bit.

Don't do what you don't love

Yeah, right. No, really. There's a whole (wheat) variety of ways to not do what you don't want to:

Just don't do it! (that's the 'Nike Says F**k It' slogan)

Sometimes we just don't do the things we think we really should. Yet, remarkably, the world keeps turning. When our boys were very little – let me see, they would have been about 18 months old – I did an experiment on toy tidying. At the time, we were living in a small flat in Balham, South London, and I was going crazy, constantly running after them and tidying the living-room floor. So I decided to not tidy at all.

The floor got progressively messier and chaotic and disgusting – if someone had visited us, we would have been ashamed, and those 'someones' might even have called in social services. But we stuck it out, because I had an idea. It was a mad idea, but it was an idea nonetheless. And the 2 per cent chance that this idea had some legs made it worth sticking with, and the pay-off would be high.

So, after x days (I don't recall how many), the floor really was beyond belief: there were toy cars, Lego, teddy bears, action figures – Christ, whatever else they had and I can't remember – all mixed up in an alphabet spaghetti of a floor covering.

The boys could hardly move for the mess. They could hardly walk. And, given that 'not walking' to 'hardly walking' to 'walking' was something they'd recently gone through, it must have been somewhat disconcerting for them to be regressing to the 'hardly walking' stage so soon.

So, maybe in a conscious attempt to assert their progression from babies to toddlers, or maybe because they wanted to teach us a lesson about how to look after a flat, or maybe because they simply thought it was a new game, the boys started to tidy up. Yes, indeed, our 18-month-old twins started to shove all the Lego into one pile in the corner, cars into another pile, teddy bears into a little gang in another corner.

In that instance, my 'not doing' something meant that the job did itself. Or rather, someone else did it. And these 'someone elses' were not people who'd resent it and moan about me behind my back. Well, at least I don't think they were – the boys haven't mentioned it since, anyway. It was a valuable lesson for me because I'm someone who likes to get things done, and keep things neat, and remain (almost) on top of things. And I think that simply 'not doing' stuff can create rather amazing results sometimes.

"""""""""""""""""""""""""""""

I was living in a student house with an unkempt garden. One day I saw that our hedge had become overrun with greenflies: the leaves were drooping with the weight of them, so it was like something from a horror film. I resolved to sort it all out soon. But the next day I forgot. The day after that I was too busy. The day after that I couldn't be bothered. Then I went away for the weekend… And then I thought, *Ah, F**k It.*

So I left the hedge, and a couple of weeks later I thought I'd better go have a look (that took some courage, as I was expecting the worst). When I did, I saw that the entire hedge was covered in ladybirds. And not just your usual red with black spots, but black with red spots, black with yellow spots, yellow with black spots. And they were ladybirds at all stages of development. It was fascinating and beautiful. And, of course, they'd eaten (and were still eating) the greenflies. Job done. Without me lifting a finger.

ISOBEL PUGH – CHESTER, UK

,,,,,,,,,,,,,,,,,,,,,,,,,,,,,,,,,,,,

Here's what can happen when you simply don't do things:

* **You end up doing it later.** But in a much more efficient way. I prefer to do tidying and washing-up after at least two meals, rather than just one. You save loads of time like this. It's Adam Smith in the kitchen.

* **Someone else does it.** Hopefully without resenting you for the rest of your life. This is Gaia's tactic on a variety of things. She's a great advocate of not doing what she doesn't feel like. Actually, I usually end up doing it, and I don't resent her for it. As long as she's doing that thing on my list that I asked her to do at this moment – the one I really couldn't face.

* **No one even notices and the thing goes away.** Many of the things we do are non-essential, and their non-essentialness becomes more apparent over time. The longer you leave the things you don't really fancy doing, the more likely it is you'll realize their uselessness in the first place. Many a time I've shuffled large piles of jobs to be done straight into the bin – six months after I so urgently needed to do them.

> ## Don't fancy doing it? F**k It: don't do it and see what happens.

If you don't fancy doing it, F**k It: don't do it and see what happens. Small print: of course, there will be things that you don't fancy doing that *are* essential. Feeding your kids is one of them. But even that… Well…

Give it to someone else

* **You can ask** – 'Gaia, can you feed the kids tonight? I know it's my turn, but pretty please.' They can always say 'no'.

* **You can delegate** – if you have that option. I do, but I'm still not good at it. It usually seems more bother to teach someone else how to do it than just do it myself. But then it takes up a lot of time, over time. So I'm trying to get better at delegating a whole raft of stuff. But I have to accept that the whole raft of stuff might not be done in the way *I* would do it. That's called 'letting go', and it's an essential F**k It quality. We don't have to let go of a task *completely* – we don't want someone to fuck it up, after all – just enough to let go of it and for someone else to do it.

* **You can outsource it** – if you have that option. This is the direct-pay version of delegation. You're delegating to someone whom you're paying specifically to complete that task. For small businesses (like ours) it's possible, and wise, to outsource a whole range of stuff. Here's a little list of what we do (or have) outsource(d):

  * *All administrative tasks* – taking bookings for retreats, issuing invoices, answering emails, etc., and that's a huge bloody ETC.

  * *Marketing tasks* – we've used PR agencies to get PR, and a social media agency to look after all our social media.

  * *Content creation* – this book is being written by a Virtual Assistant in India. Actually, content creation is one of the things that I clearly love, so I do most of it myself. But I'm working with someone at the moment who edits all our audio material (Hi Roi). And in the past, I've hired people to help create videos for us.

  * *Accountancy* – our accountant does the accounting. We don't.

Beyond the business, the domestic realm is clearly a key area in which to look for help. We have a gardener who comes once a week and a cleaner twice a week. Whenever we're looking at ways to reduce our expenses, I always go to the cleaner first and cut her hours – even though the cost of hiring her is a relatively small part of our budget. But later I always realize why it's so important to have that help, as we're soon stuck downstairs doing the washing-up rather than upstairs doing €300 Skype coaching sessions.

In fact, since the idea of hiring a cleaner comes up a lot, let's look at this one in a little more detail. Domestic work is often something that people don't particularly want to do, but feel obliged to. Even though the issue can be solved by hiring a cleaner, many people (even those with ready access to the funds) don't do that. Or they ask a cleaner to work for just one morning a week, and then spend a significant amount of the rest of the week doing the housework themselves. So I'll mention two obstacles to doing what we don't love less in the context of hiring a cleaner.

* **Mentality**: you might feel guilty about hiring a cleaner because you feel that *you* should be doing the work, and that it's very spoiled to have a cleaner. F**k It, get over it. You're giving someone else work. You deserve to do what you fancy. Get over it and call that cleaning agency right now. Or you might think that cleaning is demeaning work, almost like slave labour (really, I've heard this argument before). It's not: it's a job like many other jobs. Some people who do it will be happy doing it, others won't. Our current cleaner had been unable to find any work for years, and she's very happy to be working now. F**k It, get over it.

* **Resources**: of course there will be some readers who really
  can't afford a cleaner (see earlier reference to the current
  financial climate). But there will also be many who *think*
  they can't afford it, but, at a push, actually could (even when
  we've not been particularly flush,
  we've had a cleaner). It may well mean
  cutting back – not having that meal
  out, or those takeaways, or not
  upgrading your iPhone – but having a
  cleaner (especially if you don't really like doing the
  housework) is a huge gift to yourself. And it is usually worth
  the push. It introduces a level of abundance to your life, no
  matter what financial state you're in.

> *Oh, F**k It, just hire a cleaner.*

Oh, F**k It, just hire a cleaner. It could be the quickest way to doing
less of what you don't love and creating some time to do what you
do love.

F**K IT, I DESERVE IT.

*This F**k It Push Mantra: You do. Don't argue.
Just take it from me. And now say it again
and again until you start to believe it.*

Do what you don't particularly love in less time

So if you *have* to do something yourself – if none of the above work,
and you really just have to do it – then do it as quickly as you can.

It's funny, isn't it – well, not so funny in reality – the way we tend to
really drag out the things we don't enjoy, and procrastinate endlessly.
This is 'bad' procrastinating by the way. But there's also 'good'
procrastinating, which is recognizing that something doesn't need to

be done just yet (if at all), dropping it to the bottom of the list and not thinking about it until you need to.

'Bad' procrastinating is when you're trying to do something, but can't, and keep putting it off; however, you keep thinking about it, and beating yourself up, and generally use a huge amount of energy. Bad, bad procrastinator, you.

(Last parenthetical side point on this subject: the 19th-century proverb 'Procrastination Is The Thief Of Time' – and I Capitalize That As The Victorians Would Have Done – was referenced by Oscar Wilde in his own superior aphorism: 'Punctuality Is The Thief Of Time'. Beautiful.)

Loving doing an undesired task speedily is like layering whipped cream over a dry biscuit.

We do the job very slowly: stopping and starting, getting distracted, getting up to make a snack, or to catch some *essential* email or news. Bad girl/boy. Stop it. Do the opposite. Get the job done in the fastest possible way you can – it makes sense, doesn't it? Make speed and efficiency in the face of your undesired task something you love (like layering whipped cream over a dry biscuit).

How to do it? Well, the following techniques apply just as well to doing stuff you love really productively, as to doing the stuff you don't love, quickly:

Set unrealistic deadlines

I use this technique daily, mainly in managing my emails. I get a huge number of emails, and it's hard to delegate the answering of them to others. And, anyway, I do like to reply personally to many of the emails I get: it's a joy of the job. But if I dawdled my way through my inbox every day, it would be all I'd do.

So instead, I note down the number of emails I have, split between my inboxes (for example, I might have 45 emails in one box and 37 in another), and the timeframe I have available to answer them. Then I set the task for myself. In this example, that might be 'reply to all 82 in two hours'. Or 'reply to 45 within an hour'. And off I go.

The fastest average I have is one email per minute. The last few emails always take the longest. And I tend to have around a dozen emails that linger in the ashtray of my inbox for ages… usually until they're irrelevant and I can either delete them or write to the sender and say, 'I've just seen this, and realized that it's no longer relevant, sorry.'

Often, I don't hit my target, but what matters is the increase in speed and productivity that my method gives me. It may mean that if you send me an email, you will receive only a short reply from me, but most people get used to that.

I learned this method from Martin Sorrell, the head of WPP (the world's largest communications services group). I remember sending him an email a long time ago (I don't mean that he hasn't answered it yet, but that this was in the 1990s), asking a question, and his response was simply 'Y, M' (i.e. 'Yes, Martin').

I loved this. It was the early days of email, and a lot of people were writing them in the way they'd written letters. This was before the abbreviatory language that SMS texting introduced, too. To receive an email response that was so minimal, so pared down to the bare letters, so fat-less, delighted me. And I never looked back. I must have saved months of my life by writing fat-free emails.

For that matter, I must have saved months, or even years, by being able to touch type. When I left university (where I'd hand-written almost everything, as it was the 1980s), I did so with an Amstrad 95812 word processor in the boot of my car. I went home and asked my mum (who used to be a secretary) to teach me how to touch type. It took me two days to learn a method that has saved me so much time and effort. As I'm writing this book, I can type just about as quickly as I can think.

I started using the 'set unrealistic deadlines' technique seven or eight years ago, when I realized I was spending more time than was necessary on a particular task. I was having to re-do the website for our retreats business, 'The Hill That Breathes', and, whenever I started to think about it, I imagined it would take me a couple of months to plan it, and write it, and choose the photos, and brief it.

Setting unrealistic deadlines is real F**k It productivity.

In fact, it was taking me much longer because, knowing it would take so long, I never really got down to it. It was like looking up at Everest from base camp. And, rather than getting a piggyback from a Sherpa, I'd just go and find a nice hotel and have a lie-in instead. One day, I got so bored with my struggle and procrastination, I said to myself, *Right, lad* (I always call myself lad in my head), *why don't you just get yourself sat down, and do this bloody thing in two days?*

What? 'lad' replied. *But… but… planning the look of the homepage alone will take me two days* – which indeed it had, as I'd spent endless hours doodling various designs for homepages that would frame the images just so…

No lad, you have half an hour to do that bit. And after 'lad' had soiled his pants, and cleaned himself up, he got down to it. And, sure enough, with that ridiculous deadline, his progress was fast. Maybe not two days fast, but certainly three or even four days fast. And certainly not two or three months slow.

Provided you don't panic and worry yourself silly – i.e. you understand the game you're playing with yourself – setting unrealistic deadlines is real F**k It Productivity. For me, it means I'm doing multiples of what I used to do. It means I'm working two or three or even 10 times faster than I used to.

And, as well as increasing your speed, it (usually) improves the quality of what you're doing. Projects, and decisions, rarely benefit from hanging about and over-thinking. It also slaps self-doubt and self-criticism round the face with a wet fish. There simply isn't time to doubt and deliberate too much – just get on with it and finish it, lad.

Set rewards (carrot)

Ricardo Semler, the inspirational Brazilian business owner who invites his employees to decide on their own hours and salaries, suggests that if you've made enough widgets for the week by Wednesday, then don't go making more widgets – go to the beach instead.

I'll do that myself this week. I have five days put aside to write: today (Monday) to Friday. Then I have a workshop on Saturday. I have a target number of words to write (which takes me to the end of the book – no, I'm not writing this book in order, by the way). So I've divided that number of words by the five days: I've allowed some easing off on the fourth day, but it's pretty much divided.

If I take my own advice now, this is what I should do: divide the number of words target by four days instead of five, write faster, and take Friday off if I finish on time. Then, on Friday, I can do what the heck I fancy: I can visit a gallery, or go to the cinema; I can eat a burger and chips in a yummy gourmet burger bar, or catch a matinee theatre production. Shit, I'm writing faster already.

I often create little rewards for myself. I don't go to the beach very often once I've finished a job though, and I should do it more. Because it works.

> *With the help of F**k It, time can be your friend.*

Set punishments (stick)

I tend to prefer carrots to sticks. But maybe the threat of a good thrashing would work for you? For example, you might withhold something from yourself if you don't make your deadline: 'I won't buy that dress I like if I can't get this done.'

So, after that little lot above, time should no longer be your enemy. With the help of F**k It, time can be your friend once more.

FINDING THE MONEY

A lack of money is a fundamental reason why a lot of us don't do what we love.

If you love yoga, and want to become a yoga teacher, it's going to cost you a few thousand pounds to train – and you might not have the cash. If you love studying Sanskrit and want to do a PhD in it, you might not have the money to dedicate yourself to study. If you love Indian furniture and would love to set up a shop selling it, you might not have the money to buy your first stock.

When I was at university I had a hobby that I loved: windsurfing. But, for a student, it was an expensive hobby. So I decided to live on very little, work in the holidays, and spend the remaining pennies from my grant and pay packet on windsurfing equipment.

One summer I managed to save up to fly to a windsurfing mecca – Lanzarote, one of the Spanish Canary Islands – where I rented a tiny apartment. The thing was, I didn't have money for food, so I lived mainly on bread and butter for a month. I loved windsurfing so much that I found a way to do it.

Many people who start businesses do so without much capital to invest. So they go to the bank for a business loan. That's one of the reasons banks exist. I know that these days we think they exist to over-reward people who take huge risks on invented financial instruments, or to charge us for exceeding our overdraft limit, but a fundamental function of a bank is to help fund small businesses.

If we have a great idea for a project and need funding for it, we can usually find a way to do it. Back in the 1990s, I saw an investment opportunity but I didn't have the cash to invest. And I knew no bank would lend me the kind of money I needed for such a venture. So I opened several bank accounts (okay, 10) and took out small overdrafts. I quickly paid off those overdrafts (that improves your credit rating and thus your ability to borrow more next time), and then went back to borrow more, which I quickly paid back before going back for more. And so on, until, across the 10 accounts, I had the sum I needed to invest.

I found my own F**k It Financial Strategy.

As soon as my investment started to pay off, I paid back those initial loans. That was my F**k It Financial Strategy. It's not something I'd recommend, mind you. I'm no financial adviser, and I'm not sure it would even be possible to do that these days, but I'm sharing the story because, if we need to raise money for something we regard as worthwhile, we can usually find a way.

Although taking out a bank loan, or remortgaging a property to create capital, are common ways to fund a new venture, many of us don't want to go down that route. Because many of us are in stable, and sometimes very well-paid, jobs, and this can make it even harder to make the jump and do what we love. We find ourselves living lives that require the money that these jobs generate – with mortgages, bills, families, holiday expenses, school fees, etc.

If you're a primary school teacher living on your own, it might be hard to imagine saving up enough money to pay for yoga teacher training – and then eventually jumping to making a living teaching yoga. But it's probably going to be a darned sight easier for you to do it than it would be for a hedge fund manager who hates her job and now wants to be a yoga teacher, but is the main breadwinner in a family that lives in a multi-million-pound house with a huge mortgage and huge private school fees,

So 'finding the money' to Do What you Love is often more like 'doing without the money' you currently earn to fund your lifestyle. The trap you feel you're in might be small or big, but it still feels like a trap. There are a thousand different situations here, but I'll share some ideas, one of which might help you in the situation you find yourself in now.

Consider the downsize

Whatever that means to you. It might just mean shifting jobs, so you're working less (or you have less responsibility) but are earning less, and need to cut your cloth accordingly. It might mean selling your house and moving to a more affordable area, to create some cash to Do What You Love. What sacrifices are you willing to make (lifestyle-wise) to do more of what you love, and be happier? What are you willing to say F**k It to?

Downsizing might be part of your plan. Or maybe you can see that all you need is a certain amount of money to get you going in the move you want to make. Maybe it's the funds to cover your yoga teacher training, and enough surplus to live on without having a steady job for six months. Work out how much you need and start putting money into a F**k It Escape Fund. When your fund is full, you can make the leap.

"""""""""""""""""""""""""""""

In 2013 I said F**k It, left my job and ran away for three months to train as a storyteller. Then I said F**k It, I'm going to sell my house and live by the sea; so I put the house on the market, and got a buyer. In 2014 I said F**k It, I'm not sure about this storytelling, I don't want to leave my house, and I need some money — so I pulled out of the house sale and decided I'd like a part-time job doing a very particular role that would allow me to work some of the time at home.

The next day I got an email from a company asking if I wanted such a job. Then I thought, how many days per week do I want to work, and how much money do I want to earn. The next day there was another email, asking me those very questions! I've been doing this part-time job for a year now. :)

SANDRA REGAN — OXFORDSHIRE, UK

,,,,,,,,,,,,,,,,,,,,,,,,,,,,

Instead of thinking 'either/or', consider 'both/and'

At the moment you may well see your current job as something you hate, and your dream idea as something you'd love. So you either stick with the job (and are miserable) or take a massive risk and make the jump to making your dream idea work (and are hopefully, therefore, happy).

But consider the 'both/and' paradigm, of which there are many variations. Can you do more of what you love within your current job? Is the problem the company you work for, rather than the job itself? If so, doing the same job for a different company could be your answer. I tried both these solutions when I was in paid work.

F**K IT, I WILL HAVE MY CAKE AND EAT IT.

*This F**k It Push Mantra: What's the point of cake
if you don't eat it? Transform this absurd idiom
into something empowering. We WILL eat cake
(not the grubby stuff that Marie Antoinette was
probably referring to: no, proper cakey cake).*

My first job was with my dream advertising agency, BBH — which had been the most creative agency of the previous 10 years. But I wasn't happy there. I wondered if I'd made a huge mistake in choosing that line of work. But I moved to another agency, HHCL (which was later voted the most creative agency of the 10 years that followed), with a very different culture, and was as happy as Larry for many years.

When I started to feel a little less happy than lucky old Larry, and wanted to start experimenting with therapeutic work as a job, the agency was open enough to allow me to do so within the context of the business. I went from being a creative to using relaxation and trance techniques to help others come up with ideas.

Even if you can't get to Do What You Love within the context of your job, how can you get to Do What You Love *alongside* your job? By creating more time, you can start doing what you love at the same time as you do your job. Maybe once you're spending a good amount of time doing what you love (as well as what you don't), you'll be happier with the balance in your life. Maybe you'll be grateful for what your job gives you (a sense of satisfaction, status, money, etc.) and it will sit quite happily alongside whatever it is you're doing in your spare time.

Could you Do What You Love alongside your job?

And maybe if you do eventually want to make a living from doing what you love, you could simply start slowly. Don't put pressure on yourself. Do the yoga teacher training in your summer holidays, and then start to run a local class one evening a week. Then maybe go part-time at work, and teach yoga on your day off. Let doing what you love grow organically. Really start to play with how it could work for you.

Play your way to doing what you love

Our friend John Williams, author of *Screw Work, Let's Play*, is, as you'd expect, very big on play. He suggests that you don't have to work it all out laboriously before you get on and try to Do What You Love. Instead, you just start playing with what you love. In this fashion, you stay open and more flexible. You try something out and, if it doesn't work, you move on to something else, but in a playful way.

This is a very F**k It way to do things. In fact, being playful is one of the two ways we know in which people can enter the childlike 'F**k It State' – a calm alpha brain wave state. (For your information, the other way is consciously to relax.)

I like to play: I like the lightness and freedom of experimentation. But I also have a rather serious, perfectionist and planning side.

My personal approach is to mix the playing with the planning: to blend the light with the serious. Or rather, to move from one state to the other, and sometimes rather rapidly.

To me, this is the essence of the creative process. In creating anything, it's often best to be moving between states. Sometimes that can be rapid, and sometimes it's slow. For example, I might write purely creatively for 10 minutes and then go back over what I've written with a more logical and critical eye.

The two states tend not to coexist in the same moment – I can't write the random, surreal stuff at the same time as holding the critical and rational understanding – but I can happily switch between the two.

Comedian, actor and writer John Cleese, who knows a thing or two about creativity (and absurdities that really work) once said (somewhere, and I can't find where) that, when writing, you have to switch quickly between the clown and the lawyer.

So, John (Williams not Cleese) is right: play your way to doing what you love – your natural tendency will be the more rational 'lawyer' route, and the playful approach lets in the 'clown'. But I never let the clown take over completely – that would only end in tears (painted on or real).

The problem with the 'either/or' paradigm is that it keeps you stuck, and brings with it higher anxiety levels. You're either anxious because you're stuck doing nothing that you love, or you make the leap and are anxious that you can't make it work, or pay your bills.

However you do it, if you want to end up making a living from doing what you love, don't assume, as many people do, that it will be harder than doing your current paid job (assuming you have one). Many people are afraid of going it alone, and self-employment. And, clearly, it can be tough. You won't have the certainties that come with paid employment, but the rewards can go beyond increased freedom and choice about how you live your life.

The financial rewards can be huge (although clearly they will depend on what you love doing, and what market you're in). I cover that in Chapter 6, 'Making a Living from Doing What You Love'. Just don't exclude the possibility of good financial rewards in the area of doing what you love. When Gaia and I were working in advertising agencies, we made more money every year from our 'hobby projects' than from our not ungenerous (Oh Christ, John, you sound like your mum: just say 'bloody generous') salaries.

I spent a small fortune developing my 'F**k It Music'.

It's also the case that your hobby projects might make no money at all, at least in the short term, and that making money from them is not the point. I spent a small fortune on developing my 'F**k It Music' I have received some income from the music by doing gigs, but the overall balance sheet for that project is seriously in the red.

But I didn't do it for money. I did it for pleasure, and because I simply had to. And I *will* earn money over time with that project. I'm currently, two years after creating most of the music, putting together a 'F**k It Experience' online product that should generate a good (and passive) income.

Your hobby projects might also benefit your other projects, or even your paid work. The 'F**k It Music' I play during our retreats adds to the experience of them. The fact that I followed my dream and made the music allows those who follow the F**k It way to see that it's possible to do it. I doubt whether Richard Branson made any money from those mammoth balloon flights he used to do, but imagine the satisfaction he got from them. And imagine the effect the PR for those flights had on all his Virgin brands.

❝❝❝❝❝❝❝❝❝❝❝❝❝❝❝❝❝❝❝❝❝

I love singing, and after seeing a pop-up choir at the London 2012 Paralympics, I was inspired to set up my own. Although I had no training as a choir leader I said F**k It and set up a pop-up choir at work – starting small with just three people. Now the choir is 20 people strong, and recently we sang in a mass choir opera at London's Albert Hall!

MAYA TWARDZICKI – LONDON, UK

❞❞❞❞❞❞❞❞❞❞❞❞❞❞❞❞❞❞❞❞❞❞

FINDING THE MOOD

If your default mode is to struggle, stress and worry, then don't bring that into the realm of Doing What You Love. To reap all the benefits of doing more of what you love – on your levels of happiness, on your health, on your relationships and on your levels of success – then it's worth finding a different mode in which to operate around those things you love.

So don't put pressure on yourself. Don't jump from your job and suddenly have to start making a living from doing what you love. Try to see it more as play than a job. In fact, finding a different mode in which to operate could be one of the biggest benefits to you of exploring what it is you love.

An indicator of whether you're on the right track or not is how you're feeling. Are you feeling 'in flow' when you're doing what you love? Or does it feel like a struggle or hard work? Do you look forward to those times when you're doing what you love, or is it a chore (if it's the latter, it's hardly 'doing what you love', is it?). With our default mindsets, it's amazing how easily doing what we love can turn into a real grind.

F**K IT, THIS JUST FEELS RIGHT.

This F**k It Push Mantra: When the feelings fight with the thoughts, use this one to give the feelings a knuckle-duster.

That's why nurturing a healthy mindset can transform our lives — by allowing us to do more of what we love, and also switching our response to doing the things that we imagine we don't love. And there's a secret coming up. I've hidden it under the next heading, but if you suss this, you will exponentially multiply your chances of doing what you love in your life.

""""""""""""""""""""""""

My work was full of stress and strife for many months (I manage a charity with some big organizational challenges). After some reflection (and in a fit of mild desperation), instead of fighting against the challenges I was facing, I said F**k It and treated them as welcome guests in the chaos of a life well lived.

By saying F**k It and accepting things as they were, instead of trying to make them into something they were not, they went from problems to opportunities, and the situation slowly but surely moved from filled-with-stress to filled-with-inspiring-moments-of-awesomeness.

AMY BARTLETT – OTTAWA, CANADA

,,,,,,,,,,,,,,,,,,,,,,,,,,,,,,,,,,

FINDING THE VIRUS

'If you can't enjoy what you have, you can't enjoy more of it.'
RICHARD BANDLER, CO-CREATOR OF NEURO-LINGUISTIC PROGRAMMING (NLP)

Doing what you love with the help of F**k It can be like a slow-spreading virus. If you follow the steps outlined in this chapter – prioritize what you love and simply get on and do it, and reduce the amount of time you spend on doing the stuff you don't particularly want to do – you'll quickly find yourself doing a lot more of what you love.

The positive effects of doing what you love will only make you want to do more of what you love, so you're likely to give it even more priority, and continue to reduce the amount of stuff you don't love. Gentle virus, see.

> **Doing what you love in a F**k It way can be like a slow-spreading virus.**

But there's a way to make this Do What You Love virus spread much (much) quicker. There's a way to completely knock out the defences of everything in your life that stands in the way of everything being 'what you love'. And, just as the most lethal viruses are often a simple and small mutation of the virus gene, it's a simple and small change in our Do What You Love virus that makes it unstoppable.

This is the formula: we take the current virus of *Do What You Love,* and we make the following small and simple mutation to create a new virus – *Love What You Do.*

No new elements. No new words. No new concepts. Just a small mutation of the current formula. But this one is a real killer: if there's an area of your life where you're really struggling to Do What You Love –

because of habits, or obligations, or commitment, or whatever – when you unleash the Love What You Do virus, there's no stopping it.

Suddenly, from frustratingly being unable to Do What You Love – no matter what you try – you *are* doing it, because you're loving what you do (and as a consequence, you're now doing what you love).

So, how the heck do you unleash this new virus in your life? Well, I'd like to introduce you to someone. His name is Antonio Aloi, and I met him last summer on a trip to Salina, one of the Italian Aeolian Islands, which lie northeast of Sicily. In fact, I was so impressed by Antonio that I made notes about him at the time. Here they are, typed up from my notebook.

Antonio Aloi – the street cleaner of Salina

I spotted Antonio early on in our visit, mainly because of his leanness – a 1940s, shirt-tucked-into-trousers kind of leanness – and his smiley face. Then I saw him everywhere on my morning walks – because he *was* everywhere. He walked fast and swept fast – for that is his job: to walk around town sweeping and cleaning. This morning he was ahead of me as I walked up a slight incline, breathlessly trying to catch up with him.

As I (still breathlessly) walked behind him through town, he had a black bin in one hand and a brush in the other. I watched him do what I knew he'd do – say hello to everyone and add a little comment, to which they'd reply in a similar manner.

He never lingered (he takes his job too seriously for that), and he never added a moan to his greetings – such as 'Crikey, what a terrible night that was, eh?' – although he did have reason to: last night there was a rare July storm that woke me up at 4 a.m. and had me outside making sure nothing would get wet on our covered balcony. The torrential downpour had left a right old mess in this pristine town, with battered-down blossoms from the plentiful jasmine plants stuck to the wet pavements.

So Antonio's job was to clean up before the tourists hit the streets, and I was reluctant to stop him and speak to him (knowing that he wanted to work, and also shy about doing such things). But I said F**k It and did. I told him I was writing a book about 'doing what you love' and that it had struck me he was doing what he loved.

Antonio agreed that he was. I asked him why and he said, 'Lavoro e buono', which means 'Work is good', or 'It's good to work'. I asked him why this work, in particular, and he replied, 'Non e niente' – 'It's nothing'. I told him it was clear that he was doing a good job, and he said again, 'Non e niente'. And then I left him to get on.

Antonio Aloi, the man with the alliterative name, the ever-present smile, a bright greeting for everyone, loves his work – loves work, in fact. In a town awash with millionaires who've come ashore from their yachts to spend money like water on stuff they neither want nor need, and then moan about the weather into their cocktails, give me the life of Antonio Aloi any day.

Nine months on, there are background elements to this story, and our time on Salina, that I didn't spot at the time. But I do now. Salina is famous for being the island on which the Italian film *Il Postino* (*The*

Postman) was shot. In fact, when you get off the ferry at the port and walk along the harbour, you're greeted by the film's famous bicycle, with a large photograph of the protagonist postman, played by the late Massimo Troisi.

The film is about a simple, gentle (and beautiful) man, doing his simple job: delivering the mail on a small Italian island (in fact, he has only one customer – the famous Chilean poet Pablo Neruda). I don't know how many visitors spot Antonio Aloi, as they rush from one movie landmark to another on Salina, but he is the closest thing to a real-life *Il Postino* I've ever met. And he lives on the *Il Postino*-themed island. There must be something in the water.

Antonio Aloi did not train himself into this situation. He certainly didn't go through the process of trying to work out what he loved – 'I love sweeping streets' – before setting out to make a living from it ('I must apply to the *comune* for a job sweeping the island's streets'). And he didn't nurture the state of mind of Loving What He Does. He didn't start off really hating the job, and wishing he could afford a yacht in which to sail around the beautiful islands. He just, naturally, loves what he does. Lucky him.

F**K IT, I EMBRACE THIS AS IT IS.

This F**k It Push Mantra: Ahhhhhh, just use this one repeatedly and your life will change.

Mindfulness – the Antonio Aloi way

But it doesn't mean that we're lost. Like all gurus, we can learn from Antonio Aloi. We can imitate him, and we can model him. The essence of what he does naturally – maybe because he's a simpler person than you or me – is simply being 'present' to what he does. He lives what Buddhists refer to as a 'mindful' life.

He is, naturally, mindful: fully present to 'what is'. He doesn't clutter his present reality with too many thoughts about the past or the future. And he doesn't clutter a perception of his present reality with judgement – i.e. that things are 'wrong' or 'right', 'good' or 'bad'.

It's strange that Antonio is a street cleaner, because the street of his perception is perpetually clean. Though I wrote my book *Bob the Buddha* before I met Antonio, I created a character like him as its protagonist. By living a simple, mindful life, Bob is fully awake to reality. He doesn't know it – just as Antonio doesn't know it – but he is a modern 'Buddha'. So in modelling Antonio Aloi, we can nurture such a form of 'mindfulness'.

I take my understanding of mindfulness from my own practice over the past two decades – I was taught by several Buddhists – so it might not necessarily cohere with any modern definition of mindfulness. You can start with a more formal mindfulness practice if you like. Put aside, say, 15 minutes every day to just sit and 'be'. I do my practice while I'm doing my things – whether that's driving around or sitting waiting at a bus stop. Yours can be like that too, but most people start with a more formal sitting practice.

Mindfulness is not complicated, by the way. You might not find it easy at first, but it's not complicated. Here are some guidelines:

* Just find that time. And find a quiet place where you'll be undisturbed for 15 minutes. Just sit comfortably – you could sit in a chair, or on a cushion, in a more traditional meditative pose if you want. It's best at first not to lie down,

because you're more likely to fall asleep that way. I love doing my practice standing up, but that too, at first, might be more difficult, as you'll be thinking about the position of the body, and any discomfort in the legs.

* So you're just sitting there. You don't have to think anything in particular. You don't have to imagine an Om sound. You're just noticing what's coming up for you. You're noticing any sensations in your body. You're noticing what's entering your head – whether that's thoughts, or stimuli from outside, or thoughts in response to those stimuli – 'My, that aeroplane is loud.'

* You don't *judge* these thoughts or responses. Nothing's excluded here. No thought is wrong or right, even if your thoughts are about what is wrong or right – 'They really shouldn't send aeroplanes over a built-up area – it's disgusting.'

* Your mind-body is like the sky, and thoughts and sensations are like clouds passing over that sky. You're just watching them passing. Sometimes you'll be within the clouds – not watching them, but within them – and that's fine too.

* You see? You can't really go wrong with this one. You're just sitting there for 15 minutes and noticing what's going on.

* If you want, you can add a line to the thoughts and things you notice – something like, *Ah, that's interesting.* This constitutes the 'not-judging' thing: 'Those airlines are terrible'/*Ah, that's interesting*; 'I feel sick and tired'/*Ah, that's interesting*; 'I'm so bored with this'/*Ah, that's interesting*, and so on.

Once you've done this practice for a while in such a formal (but completely relaxed) way you can start to take it out into the world. Well, the truth is that if you do this regularly enough, you won't have any choice, as it will happen naturally. Your just-watching-and-not-really-judging way of being will start to seep into everything you do, and everything you perceive.

Sure, it's not that you'll become some pure, gentle, and compassionate Buddha-like version of yourself. (Well, you might – it probably depends on how you are naturally.) And you don't have to be that. It's more that you'll add this extra 'being present' thing to your normal mix of normal responses to the 10,000 things of everyday reality.

Well in fact, it's not even an additional response – it somehow becomes present in everything. It's like a perfume that's detectable in everything you do and think. So that even in your judging, negative response to something, there's still the perfume of non-judgement in there, too.

> *We don't give up doing what we love – we simply find ourselves loving more what we do.*

And as this perfume spreads through your perceptive life, you find yourself just liking things for what they are. You find yourself 'loving' the most bizarre things, and you realize you're loving the most mundane tasks. You find yourself present when previously you would have been absent.

When you're doing something you previously didn't like, you find yourself liking it, or even loving it. And thus, mixed up somewhere in this journey to Doing What We Love, we find ourselves Loving What We Do. It's not that we say F**k It and stop pursuing, in one way or another, the idea of doing more of what we love. It's that we, in the meantime, find ourselves loving more what we do.

F**K IT, I CAN ENJOY THIS.

*This F**k It Push Mantra: Even if you think you can't, you can. And this will help that movement.*

The journey into doing more of what we love, and the present experience of loving more what we do, becomes like a dance – and it's a very good dance at that. There's no stepping on toes here; there's a synergy created by the two dancers that makes the movement and effect much more beautiful than one person dancing alone. It's the secret trick here. And it's the essence of Living By Doing What You Love, aka 'F**k It Living'.

5

LIVING BY DOING
WHAT YOU LOVE

*'You need not leave your room. Remain sitting
at your table and listen. You need not even listen,
simply wait. You need not even wait, just learn to
become quiet, and still, and solitary. The world will
freely offer itself to you to be unmasked. It has
no choice; it will roll in ecstasy at your feet.'*

FRANZ KAFKA

Now this chapter will probably feel as if it
doesn't fit. You see, the rest of the book is
for adults, and you know already that I'm not
referring to its pornographic content (as there
is none). Or at least the rest of the book is
for the adult part of us, which for most of us
is the biggest part.

But there's a part of us that probably got left
behind, way back when most other people were
bigger than us, and there was less hair around
our armpits and private bits. You see, much of
this book works with what we've *become* –

rational, planning, strategizing, objective-led, obligation-bound adults – and explores how F**k It can help sort out that adult part of us. But in this chapter we're going to be playing with our less adult, less rational side.

Don't worry though, adult you. We're not going to be doing stupid, childish exercises, or finger-painting or pretending to be lions or anything. Well, probably not, anyway. If the lion thing happens spontaneously, it's nothing to do with me.

And don't worry though, adult you, Part II. I won't be suggesting you hand over your life to a more spontaneous, childlike side of you. No way, José. We're not going to hand over the car keys to the kids. But we're at least going to see what it's like to have them sitting on our knee and pretending to drive.

We might let them try to negotiate a corner or two as well, but we'll be right there with our hands poised, ready to correct them. Jeez, you're so RESPONSIBLE, you are.

Right, I'm listening to music whilst writing this. Rather loud music, actually. And each track, with its different quality, brings out something different in me. The current song is by Fedez

– a brilliant and funny Italian rapper – who opens it by propositioning a prostitute: not in that way, but by asking her if she'll marry him and have his kids. You must hear it.

Now this track is so 'up' that I need to jump around a bit. Which I will. Hold on a moment. Thanks, I'm back now. Shit, it's off again; this is brilliant. Hold on a moment. Right, I'm back – a little breathless, but back.

So, before we get deep into this subject, pull some music into your life. Find new music. Rediscover music you haven't listened to for years. (I use Spotify, which makes this all much easier.)

This morning I read an email from someone who has just been to see the 1980s punk-rocker Billy Idol in Australia (they live there: they didn't go all the way 'down under' just to catch him – that would be taking this Do What You Love thing way too far, wouldn't it?) and it reminded me of my first year as a driver.

Back in 1984 I had a rather fast little Mini – well, it felt fast to me, in the way a go-kart would feel fast on a motorway – and the soundtrack to that year was Billy Idol's album *Rebel Yell* (particularly the track *Eyes*

Without a Face, which has the most amazing guitar riff). I pulled that album up on Spotify in two seconds flat, and it took me all the way back to 1984. Everything came flooding back – and I mean EVERYTHING.

So sort the music thing out today. It will probably be a key part of getting this 'living by doing what you love' thing to work.

SPONTANEOUS, BLANK-PAGE LIVING

Okay, so I'm going to let you in on a bit of my process now. I'm sitting here on a Saturday morning with a big blank page…

…which has the title of the chapter, 'Living By Doing What You Love', written at the top, and a quote, but nothing else. Oh, apart from the note '12,000 words', which is my estimate of how much I'd like to write for this chapter.

The way I'd normally go about writing those 12,000 words, as you can probably guess from other parts of this book, is by chunking everything down into small sections and points that lead logically from one to the next – making an argument and a larger point and hopefully giving you great ideas and processes for saying F**k It and getting to do more of what you love.

> *I prefer to say, 'F**k It: feel the fear of that blank page.'*

But I'm resisting that route now. I'm resisting the careful planning of it all. I'm resisting the pull of the reassuring 24 or so points, with 500 words each. Because I prefer to say, 'F**k It: feel the fear of that blank page' (that A2 page with a distinct absence of notes), and I type away into this Word document, the vastness of the empty pages beneath me.

I'm not used to it – this vast emptiness. Just as I'm not used to having empty days any more. My days are planned and scheduled – even now that I'm able to spend a lot longer at home, I still use my various systems to get the most out of my days. Even now that I spend a good amount of time eating with my family, or watching TV with the boys, or napping, or walking, it's still very scheduled.

Yes, really. I will usually schedule the whole day out, just like this:

Morning
8–9. Qigong and breakfast.

9–11. Write/respond to emails.

11–12. Write the magazine article.

12–1:15 Skype coaching call.

Afternoon/evening

1:15–3. Pick boys up from school, eat lunch, watch an episode of *How I Met Your Mother*.

3–4. Relax and have a nap.

4–5. Go for a walk.

5–7. Work on new e-course.

7–8. Prepare and eat dinner.

8–10. Watch TV with the family. Yes, again… really.

So you might read that and go: 'Wow, I wish I could live like that.' Or: 'Christ, how boring.' Or: 'They watch too much TV, those Parkins.'

But it's pretty clear that I don't go overboard on the work thing; there's also no time wasted commuting, and I have a pretty balanced life… with plenty of downtime.

But… But…

There's still no real 'blank-page' time in my day, though, is there? In fact, that blank-page time is, literally, precluded by my filling in part of a page with that exact schedule. So, why do I do it? To protect that downtime: to use my work time most productively; to know where I am, and know where I'm going.

Which is all good, but still there's no blank-page time there. There's no time when I don't know what the hell I'm going to do, like now. No time when I don't have a plan – when I'm aimless, slightly scared, and verging on 'bored'. And that's a very different state of affairs from when I was short and hairless.

So, let's both go on a journey back in time, and see what we used to get up to.

Back to the short and hairless era

So, before I start describing some of my experiences, pause for a second yourself and cast your mind back to when you were a child. What did you used to get up to?

I'm instantly looking back at the school holidays, so maybe you can start there, too. In fact, I'm being transported back to sitting in front of the television around 40 years ago, 1975, watching the opening credits of a children's programme called *Why Don't You?* Now this show's kid-sung-theme-song contained a peculiar invitation: to NOT WATCH the programme – to turn off the TV and go and do something less boring instead!

I realize now that this song was probably very influential for me: because it was just WRONG. A TV programme, with all the money that's been lavished on its production – and as this was a BBC programme, that would have been TV licence-payers money... mind you, the clip of the show I've just watched on YouTube suggests that not a lot of their money was spent – and with all the great intentions they must have had for primetime holiday viewing, and they start the show by saying – 'DON'T WATCH THIS, IT'S BORING: GO AND DO SOMETHING MORE INTERESTING INSTEAD.'

An invitation NOT to watch a show: that's real F**k It TV programming.

WOW. That's real F**k It TV programming. And, you know what, half the time I would take them up on that invitation. I'd switch off the TV, wander outside and try to find something to do. The other half of the time I would watch the show. And I remember sitting there, watching kids my age presenting the show, wondering how the heck they had the courage to go on TV. I was shy, you see. I found walking into a room full of kids or adults tough to do – never mind talking on TV to millions of viewers.

But that invitation NOT to watch the show was astonishing, and it still surprises me. I don't think it was a form of reverse psychology on the part of the producers – 'Don't watch this, don't watch this', until you can't do anything else but watch it. No, it was part provocation (like punk TV) – 'We don't give a shit if you don't watch this', with the swagger of cocky seven-year-olds who could take over a TV programme – and part honesty: 'They're just pointing a camera at us kids as we talk nonsense, which can be pretty boring really, can't it? Well, F**k It.'

F**K IT, WHO CARES IF IT'S WRONG?

*This F**k It Push Mantra: In a world of tight conformity, scripted, on-brand soundbites and tight-arsed perfectionists, release your hold on excellence and open to stuff you do being wrong.*

Telling people not to watch your TV show is NOT something you do. It was wrong, and thus it was refreshing. It stood out and lives on in my head to the point where it's the first memory I'm transported back to as we do this. (A TV show like that wouldn't be made today

– you know, that don't you? Not in these over-researched, over-analysed, over-accountable, over-regulated days. Even the world of children's TV has grown up.)

I'm back in the 1970s again now, and I'm out in the garden –

I'm doing really high swings on our double swing, and then jumping off when it reaches its greatest height… I'm trying to persuade my sister to put her foot under the metal leg of the swing – which rises from the ground as the swinging person swings one way, and then slams back into the ground as they swing back – and probably lose it in the process…

Now I'm lying on the grass, looking up at the sky and hearing distant planes overhead….

I've taken the darts out of the shed and my mate Phil and I decide to play the game of *How far can you throw a dart?* His first throw ends with a loud metallic sound, followed by shouting from next door – he's hit our neighbours' brand new caravan… now I've taken the axe from the shed and I'm staging a ceremony with three friends (Phil, Jonathon and Theresa), in which we each have one swinging slice at the apple tree in my garden, before handing the axe to the next person.

We do this until my dad's car rumbles into the driveway and we scarper. But our work is discovered (and the half-chopped apple tree never really recovers)… and the total mind-blowing excitement of the paddling pool… and the standing on the wall waiting for a sweet from the milkman… and the climbing into an abandoned house in the park, knowing that it was dangerous and wrong and loving it all the same….

And... do you know what I'm doing? I'm scanning – and relating to you – the 'best of' memories. The bits that stand out now. The 40-year-old experiences that changed something in my brain – that burned their mark on my neural synapses.

What's missing – what's now a blank page in my head – is the 99 per cent of moments that weren't noteworthy enough to burn their mark on my brain. You see my brain is – and always has been – prejudiced. It selects and stores based on certain criteria. And if the experience doesn't match the criteria, it's tossed away.

So today I can only guess at those 'blank-page moments' of my childhood – the sitting around being bored, the sad times, the total absence of any conscious thoughts or reasoning as I stared at the grass or into the sky, or at a caterpillar crawling across a leaf. Or the total immersion in something; licking the salt and vinegar off a chip; dividing a piping hot lasagna, to allow it to cool down; fantasizing about a bike with three gears.

In fact, even in that process, I started to uncover actual memories that were buried just below the surface, below the headline memories. So maybe they're all there after all.

But here's the thing (aha, a POINT) – during those long summer holidays (or the shorter Easter ones), for most of my childhood, even into my teens – I had no agenda. My days were blank pages. I'd wake up and not know what the day would hold. I wouldn't wake up every day and immediately start to think about what I had to do, or how I could get the most out of the day. Once I'd started living the day, I wouldn't be constantly assessing either the utility of what I was doing (purpose) or the enjoyment I was gaining from it (pleasure).

F**K IT, I'M HAPPY TO DO NOTHING.

*This F**k It Push Mantra: Because I rarely do nothing, this one really works for me. It allows me to extend the time I spend doing nothing before I recommence doing something. This mantra multiplies nothing (apologies to the mathematicians out there, who know that you don't then get any more nothing, as I'm suggesting you would).*

Okay, so maybe that life – the past – is now a 'foreign country' to me. But, F**k It, I've got a passport. And even if I only get to visit the tourist sites, and eat in the tourist restaurants from a tourist menu, I want to make that trip and see what I can learn.

I even want to bring some of that 'foreign country' into the land of the present, as an adult. Hopefully it will be less like a tacky souvenir of a donkey to hang on a wall, and more like bringing back a new and exotic recipe that spices up our meals occasionally.

The past is a 'foreign country': but, Fk It, I've got a passport.**

So what the hell was I doing back then? What were *you* doing back then? Without the agenda, the to-do list, the long-term purpose, the crowding daily obligations, the grinding routine… what made me/you put one foot in front of the other and do something?

It's weird doing this, isn't it? We're like scientists trying to understand a foreign species. Stripped of their daily routine and schedules, what did these creatures do all day? And WHY did they do it? Well, we were just living. Spontaneously. Without questioning and without analysing. Here's what I was doing:

I'd get up and feel like watching TV so I'd go downstairs and watch the cartoons for a while; I'd feel hungry so I'd get myself a bowl of cornflakes with milk; I'd get bored watching TV so I'd head off to my mate Phil's house, knock on the door and see if he was around. His mum would usher me up to his bedroom, which was a total TIP, where he'd still be asleep. But half an hour later we'd be standing in his greenhouse, wondering what to do.

And I'd be wishing that I was as old as Phil was – it was so cool, being nine rather than seven – and he'd tell me a story about what a friend had done at school; and then he'd suggest making a slingshot so we could see who was best at knocking over cans with stones. Before I knew it there would be a call from my mum to say lunch was ready. And before I knew it again, it would be time for bed, and another chance to be barred from watching *Starsky and Hutch* – oh, how I longed to watch *Starsky and Hutch*, but it started at 9 p.m. and that was bedtime.

Foreign country, see?

But I was living spontaneously as a kid. And I was living by doing pretty much what I fancied from moment to moment. I had no agenda, no plan, no obligations. Just a blank page of a day that I'd fill spontaneously, as the whim would take me – pretty much as I'm doing with these words now.

And that blank-page living meant that I'd have bored moments (*What should I do now?*); I'd have 'blank' moments, where I'd just disappear; I'd have 'peak' experiences (like my mate's dart hitting the neighbours' caravan). I was, in modern-spiritual-speak, fully 'present' and in the now. But I didn't have to read a book called *The Power of Now* to be in the now. I didn't have to meditate to be present. In fact, from a kid's viewpoint, the idea of sitting still and trying to be present seems completely absurd.

In many ways, as kids we were enlightened without knowing it. Little Buddhas without a clue – well, having sussed the biggest clue, but without a clue that we'd sussed it. Because we just WERE.

> *When we were kids, we didn't have to meditate to be 'present'.*

That was the Garden of Eden. And it's only now that we're locked out of it that we see how blissful it was – that total moment-by-moment innocence. Only when it's gone do you see what you've lost. Well, in this context, I think we're actually lucky that we can see what we've lost, because we can try to get some of it back.

TIME AND A QUESTION

So, how do we do that? Well, it's easier than you might think actually, old man/woman. It comes down to two things: Time and a Question. And guess what's going round my head now? It's *A Question of Time*: do di do di da da, do di do di da da. (What – you don't get it? It's a song by Depeche Mode, my goodness.)

Are these constant asides frustrating you? Is the rambling style frustrating you? Would you like me to just get to the frickin' point? If so, this chapter is, more than any other part of this book, for you. The more it frustrates you, the more it's *for* you.

Because this blank-page living is accompanied by a good amount of aimless rambling, and barely remembered jokes and references, and random ideas. It's a day-dreamy way of thinking that, while frustrating for the on-purpose, highly focused adult in you, is the highly fertile soil for a few very interesting plants:

* Peak, unexpected experiences.

* Unsearched-for happiness.

* 'Spiritual' insights.

But first, let's return to those two points – those two portals back into a more childlike, spontaneous way of living – Time and a Question.

Time

Time first, then. Why did you have so much time as a kid, to get up when you wanted and do whatever you fancied for the whole day (during the holidays at least)? I'll draw on my own family's lifestyle back in the 1970s as an example (although this gender-divided paradigm has changed somewhat since then):

My dad would go to an office for most of the day (remember we last saw him pulling into the driveway, where my friends and I had just been chopping down his prize apple tree), and in return for doing so he was given special 'tokens' that paid for the car that drove him to and from the nice detached house we lived in; they paid for the house itself, and all the furniture in it too, including my bed; they paid for my toys and my bike, and all the food that we ate, all the gas that heated my bedroom in the winter, and the electricity that lit our garish carpets and wallpaper.

After waking up, my mum would immediately start readying the way for her husband and two children: cooking food, preparing clothes, packing lunches, stuffing handkerchiefs into sleeves. And she'd pretty much do that kind of stuff until it was time to go to bed again: cooking, cleaning, preparing, polishing, tidying, dusting, supervising, clearing-up-after, buying provisions, preparing provisions, eating provisions, clearing away mess from eating of provisions – on and on and on.

In the evenings, the ever-present Sony TV was watched by the three of us while sitting on the sofa, and by Mum as she stood at the ironing board she'd set up behind us. She never asked us to do a thing. So we didn't. The horror of it. Thanks, Mum.

And that, you stunted, hairless, spoiled little brat, is why you had so much time to do what the fuck you fancied for days, weeks and years on end. The Garden of Eden clearly must have had Mr and Mrs God working all hours in the background, cleaning up after Adam and Eve. And what thanks did they get? Well, not much.

They even went to that tree they weren't supposed to and ate the app… Oh, my God, I've just realized my chopping down the apple tree tale is part of my own 'Fall' story. If only I'd left that axe alone – maybe I'd still be living in the Garden of Eden.

So, yes, having Time is an essential part of being able to live more spontaneously, more like a kid. But how the heck do we create such Time, now that we don't have Mummy and Daddy any more? Well, there are two factors here:

* Creating more spare time.

* Not filling that time with plans and goals, or your default escapist crap.

Ironically, one of the reasons you have so little spare time – and when you do have it, you fill it with planned stuff or escapist crap – is that your mum and dad set a bad/good example. By being so good, and working so hard to create a supportive, stable environment for you to piss around in as you pleased, they showed you how 'good' adults should behave, and you're therefore probably doing just the same yourself.

Just take me, today, as an example. It's a Saturday. The kids are at school (that's what they do in state schools here in Italy: yes, they have classes on Saturday mornings). Gaia's teaching the morning session of a 'F**k It Magic' retreat that has just started. So I'm here on my own. And will be for most of the day.

I have, unusually, finished most of my other work for the week too. So if I hadn't agreed to write this book by a certain date, I could just hang around and do fuck all the whole day. Thanks, guys.

I'd have had my blank page. I could have got up and watched some TV for a while (okay, I did that anyway); I could have played the piano, gone for a wander in the woods, read a book, had a bath, gone back to bed. Anything I bloody well wanted.

But *would* I have done that – if I hadn't had to write this book? Honestly? No, sadly not, I think. I can judge that because I haven't had a blank-page day for ages; in fact, I normally only get them when I'm on holiday.

But, why the hell not? If I wasn't writing this, there'd be a gap, and I could use that gap as I pleased. Well, but, no, but…. If I hadn't known that I had to get stuck into this chapter today, I'd probably have spread my work out a bit more earlier in the week (i.e. I knew I had to keep this morning free, so I made sure I finished urgent tasks yesterday), so I'd be doing my normal work routine at this very moment.

That's 'Parkinson's Law' actually – work will spread itself out into the space available for it. So if I think I have Saturday morning to work, then work is what I'll be doing on Saturday morning. Let's say, though, that my work is very defined and limited, and that, even working at a gentle pace this week, I'd finished it by yesterday lunchtime. Well, sadly, I'd still have found something else of a work nature to do this morning. I'd be getting ahead of myself. Or I'd be using the time to plan a new project. Or researching something important.

You see, I have a purpose-and-achievement-orientated mentality, combined with an inherited Protestant work ethic, and so I will always end up working on a Saturday morning, no matter what real work I have to do. But, let's say that I put aside this Saturday as a 'holiday', squeezed all my work into the week, and finished at lunchtime on Friday, as I did yesterday. And let's say I'm on my own, so I can do what I want.

Well, you know what, I'd likely be feeling guilty still. So I'd probably try to go for non-work activities that have some benefit or point to them. I'd start by tidying or cleaning something (there's never a shortage of those things) – for example, the cars need cleaning. Then I'd realize that I need to do something FOR ME today, but it would still probably need to have a benefit – so I'd go for a walk (exercise) or do a longer session of Tai Chi.

And let's just say I do decide to watch some TV – I might even try to watch something that, in some way, has a purpose… like a film that will teach me something, or that I can study (yes, I do study how story works, and how films are shot).

What a miserable insight into my character that little lot was (and God, I hope I have the courage to leave all that in). You see why I've become the 'F**k It Guy'? I need the F**k It thing big-time – to drag my feet off this treadmill and prise my nose from this grindstone. Christ.

Creating some spare, blank-page time

But do you see why I've given you this (sadly, hyperbolic) example of me, and today? Can you see that creating the time is probably less of a problem than how we decide to use it? But we have to start there (if there's no time to play with, we can't get on to the next point: a Question). So here are some ideas for creating some spare time, shot from the hip, in blank-page style:

> *I need F**k It to drag me off this treadmill and prise my nose from this grindstone.*

* Hire your mum and dad (again).

* Hire mum and dad substitutes. We saw what my mum and dad did. Let's start with my mum first. Not because her job was easier, but because it's probably easier for you to see how you could hire a mum replacement (and, to all mums out there, and dads, and carers and guardians: no, we're not talking about the irreplaceable loving and protecting part of what you do and are – of course not).

If you have the money, hire someone to do the tasks that you don't particularly want to do (or, even if you do, hire them anyway, as we're trying to create some blank-page time here, for God's sake): hire a cleaner; hire someone to pick up the kids from school and prepare their dinner; hire someone to prepare meals for you too, even if it's the guy who stacks pre-prepared food into an aisle at the supermarket. (Do you see how that works? Buying a nice, healthy, pre-prepared meal is effectively like hiring someone to cook for you.) Find someone to do your administrative tasks, to book your travel and holidays. This is the world of outsourcing, hiring and delegation.

Right, Dad's turn. Mmmm, not so obviously easy. You need someone or something to go out and earn some cash for you. Without you doing anything (just staying at home and chopping down apple trees). In fact, you could do with them earning cash for you 24 hours a day, not just 9–5. It doesn't have to be all the cash you need, but at least some of it. This is the world of 'passive income'; mind you, I haven't found many incomes that are entirely passive, so it's not the best term to use.

However, I do have sources of income that, with very little time input on my part, put cash in my bank account every single day of my life, at all hours. I wake up in the morning and see that cash has appeared in my account. Whilst I was sleeping. Thanks DAD (well, the cash has nothing to do with my *actual* dad: just so you know I'm not some silver-spoon trustafarian).

Rather poetically, this morning's activity – writing this book – again provides the perfect example. Here, I'm using my time to earn money (as you know, I'm not reading a novel on the lounger in the garden, or lying in the bath). The money I'm earning for this work, this morning, is an 'advance' payment from my publisher for writing this book. And if you take that total advance and divide it by the total number of hours it will take me to write it, you'll have my hourly rate for the project. None of the following figures are real, but you'll see what I mean.

So, if I was given £1,000 as an advance for this book and it took me a total of 100 hours to write it, I'd be earning an hourly rate of £10 an hour for this project. Now, let's say we're back at the point where my publisher is offering me an amount for the book. I know roughly how long it takes me to write a book of this length, and I also know roughly what I can earn doing other types of work (say, teaching Tai Chi), so I would then make a judgement as to whether it's worth it.

And that's how paid-per-hour work works. You make a judgement on what you can earn, and you try to earn as much as you can per hour, but your total earnings are always limited by the number of hours you have in your day (and my hours are limited to five or six hours, six times a week).

There are many ways to get your 'dad' working for you again.

However – and here's why this is a good example – if this book sells well and earns for the publisher more than the £1,000 they've paid me as an advance, then another way of paying me kicks in – the royalty. A royalty is a percentage of the revenue for every book sold. So if, say, a copy of the book is sold in Dundee, Scotland for £15, and I'm receiving a 5 per cent royalty, I'll be getting a royalty of 75 pence. So royalty is dad (no, my dad's not the king).

But, by the time any royalties kick in, I've long stopped writing these words. I've long stopped doing any direct work whatsoever on this book. But the book keeps working. 'Dad' keeps working. Sure, it's not that the book is selling on its own. The publisher is working hard. The bookshops are working hard. Amazon's algorithms are working hard. And, as I said, few incomes are entirely passive – I'm still doing work myself that affects the sales of my books – such as blogs, or talks, or media interviews, or sending emails to all our followers talking about the books.

But, for the purpose of this demonstration, my use of time this morning – which is being paid by the hour – will one day render a 'dad' income that won't require my time commitment. Not that it's easy. Most books don't sell in sufficient quantities to 'earn out' the advance paid to their authors. Most books don't generate much in the way of royalties. But those that do are creating incomes for their authors.

And it's the same for songs. I know people who are living and eating and holidaying on the proceeds of work that they did in the 1980s. Noddy Holder, frontman of British 1970s glam rock band Slade, earns an estimated £500,000 a year in royalties from the band's 1973 hit *Merry Xmas Everybody*. Sting has earned £10million JUST for one song he wrote and recorded with his band The Police: *Every Breath You Take* (which appears to be a love song, but is actually a message from a stalker to his prey – which is kind of 'wrong' and, again, a reason for its success).

But you don't have to be an author or a songwriter to earn 'dad' income. You could be a business owner who finds other people to run your business; or a property investor who borrows money to buy property, and then lets it out, and the rent pays for the interest on the loan and much more; or a wise investor who chose the right stocks and is now living off the income; or an inventor who patented an interesting technology or development.

There are many ways to get your dad working for you again. And with a combination of finding a dad to earn income for you whilst you sleep, and a mum to do the tasks that fill up your time, you can create large amounts of spare time – just like you had when you were a kid.

* **And on a less ambitious scale, simply find ways to create more spare time in your life.** We talked about this earlier in 'Finding the time', but it could be about working more efficiently, or deciding there are things that you really don't have to do (and the world won't come to an end).

Let's say that you've created your spare time – a little or a lot. And let's say that you're able to keep it spare, and not fill it with either new projects or escapist crap. Now we get to the second part of our simple two-step, how-to-live-from-doing-what-you-love guide:

A question

Ask yourself the following question: 'What do I fancy doing?' Or 'What do I feel like doing?' Or 'What would I love to do now?' Or… whatever wording you fancy along these lines.

F**K IT, WHAT DO I FANCY?

This F**k It Push Mantra: The killer mantra that can take you from being a human automaton being run by other people – and all the shoulds and the oughts – to an instinctive, spontaneous, living human being.

Now this may well sound simple. Too simple. But I've worked with it for a long time. Asking yourself this question (or the correctly worded one for you) can be like having the keys to the kingdom (or the entry back into the Garden of Eden). This book is called *F**k It – Do What You Love*, and the key to doing what you love can be (is) as simple as asking yourself, 'What would I love to do?' and then saying F**k It and doing it.

Is it really that simple? Yes, kind of. In that, if you follow this through, and practise it in the way I'm about to suggest, and keep asking this question, and keep saying F**k It and following it, until you build in a new way of being (into your being) – a new and spontaneous way of living which, with the positive, astonishing results it can elicit, locks this behaviour into your psyche – then yes, it can be that simple.

> ## Ask yourself: 'What would I love to do?' Then say F**k It and do it.

So find your wording to the question now. In order to remain consistent with the title of this book, for me the question should be: 'What would I love to do?' But I've worked for so long with this wording, 'What do I feel like doing?', that I'll stick with it as I take you through this chapter.

The question 'What do I feel like doing?' has been at the heart of the teaching on our F**k It Retreats here in Italy for 10 years. The core process that we teach – and this is so memorable for all those who've attended a retreat – involves asking this question again and again.

Shake it, baby!

I'm now going to explain what we do on the retreats, and get you straight into it – so you can practise it yourself – and then guide you through how to spread it out into every moment of your life. This exercise is the magic gateway back into a more childlike and spontaneous way of living – this is the wardrobe that will take you into a Narnia way of living, but usually without the White Witch getting in the way and ruining everything.

Okay, fasten your seatbelt. Actually, no, don't fasten your seatbelt – that's the last thing you should be doing. Undo your seatbelt and get up.

First, put on some music. Ideally this will be a playlist of songs that's around 30 minutes long and features some carefully chosen tracks that match the changes in rhythm that we'll need over the half-hour of this exercise; it also needs to hit the right emotional notes at the right time, and mean something personal to you. I've given you a link to this perfect Do What You Love playlist formula in the One-Page Appendix, along with a few playlists I made earlier too.

But for now:

1. Put on some music with a good enough rhythm that you can shake your body to it.

2. Start shaking your body to the music. Now I say 'shaking' as flippantly as if I'd used the word 'dancing', don't I? I say it as flippantly as I remember B.K.S. Iyengar did in his hugely influential text *Light on Yoga*, as he went from '1. Stretch down to touch your toes.' TICK. To '2. Bend your knees slightly.' TICK. To '3. Place your head on the floor.' WHAT?

I know that 'shaking' is not normally something we naturally think of doing when we hear music, but I want you to have a go now. Hold on, let me go to Spotify, and show you the kind of thing I mean. Right,

The Chemical Brothers' *Another World* is playing. And I'm up (and popping back frequently to type this), shaking out my arms first, as if I'm shaking the water off my hands after doing the washing-up.

Then I'm shaking my whole body – bouncing on my heels, shaking all the way through my body. I'm shaking my shoulders like mad: trying to shake every cell, getting to every bit of tension in my body… My, I feel better… I've been sitting here all day, tapping away, so being able to get up and shake it out is really very good.

3. Keep shaking. You can't shake too much (certain medical conditions, slipped discs etc., excepted). You'll know if you have anything that makes shaking a bad idea, and if you do, don't.

4. At a suitable point, and I'd say an obvious suitable point would be at the end of the second song you play – so you've been shaking for about eight minutes – STOP.

5. And stand still. Notice what's going on inside your body. And your head. Yup, just notice. See if you can put words to what you're noticing. Those words might include *I'm warm*; *There's some tingling*; *I'm tired*; *That bit aches*, and so on.

6. Start shaking again. We're only going to be shaking for one song this time, so really make the most of it. I could give you lots of exercises to do at this point (they'd be 'Qigong' exercises), but most of you wouldn't read them, or do them, and you'd just skip this chapter because it's too complicated, so we're sticking with the shaking. Though in truth the shaking is as good as any exercise you can do anyway, so enjoy these four or so minutes of shaking.

7. As the song is coming to an end, really go for it: make the shaking as vigorous as you can – even if it whacks you out – as you'll be able to stand still again soon.

8. Stop. And stand still. You can leave the music playing, as we'll need it again in a minute. Once more, notice how you're feeling, and what's going on in your head. And try to relax.

9. Yeah, really try to relax as you stand still there. Relaxing means softening any tension in the body. It means letting go of anything you're holding on to. It means dropping those shoulders some more. It means softening the focus of your eyes. It means slackening your jaw (which naturally, without any effort, will also slacken your pelvis). A good tip for women giving birth that one – though go easy on the shaking if you're about to do that. Relax and relax and relax. And continue to notice (and name) how you're feeling.

There should be plenty of tingling and warmth going on here. And if there's not, please seek medical attention immediately. Noooo, not really… we all feel things differently, and even if you've actually got something going on, it might well be that you're so unaccustomed to tuning in to what you're feeling, you can't actually feel it.

On retreats, when we ask someone how they're feeling – *what* they're feeling – it's not uncommon for them to be unable to answer… they aren't feeling a thing: nothing about temperature or sensations… just nothing.

10. A good number (though '9' was too; don't feel left out, dearest 9). Now THE QUESTION kicks in: 'What do I feel like doing?'

I I. And an answer should hopefully kick in pretty soon after. The music is on. You're all shaken, possibly stirred. An answer will pop up as naturally as a fart bubble in a fresh warm bath. What's your answer to the question 'What do I feel like doing?' I get the feeling it will be one of these:

* Bending over.

* Stretching that bit.

* Shaking that bit some more.

* Yawning.

* Lying down.

* Putting my head on the floor.

* Getting into this yoga asana.

* Making this funny sound.

* Yawning.

* Shouting.

* Crying.

* Dancing to this cool music. But not my normal dance: this weird one, because no one is watching.

* Jumping.

* Jogging on the spot.

* Stretching this bit, and shaking that bit some more.

* Rubbing this bit (ooohhh matron, if you fancy it, love).

* Tapping this bit… again and again.

* Yawning.

* Crying.

* Jumping up and down.

* Dancing like they do in the Harlem Shake video.

* Gently rocking backwards and forwards.

12. Well, F**k It, bloody well do it then.

13. Then ask yourself again – 'What do I feel like doing?'

14. And do it. It won't do you any harm. It's not unlucky.

15. Just keep doing this for two or three songs… asking yourself what you feel like doing, and then just bloody well doing it… and see where it takes you. Then…

16. Stop dead still. Stop the music. And notice, again, how you're feeling.

(ASIDE: Oooohh, I've just had an idea – in this maelstrom of spontaneous, in-the-moment, doing-as-we-fancy practice – for our retreats next year. And it's a really, really good idea. Do you see how the ideas come? It's a practice like this that pops out the good ones: the things that make a difference.

This is the fertile ground I was talking about earlier – I don't get ideas by sitting at a clean desk and planning; I get them here at my messy, teacup-strewn desk, with the music loud and mixing jumping around my study tapping away for your benefit about how you can shake and move and dance and find your thing. Just by asking the question, again and again – 'What do I feel like doing?').

17. And then, just like fucking magic – no fucking asterisks there my friend, as this is fucking amazing – as I typed '17', my previous more dancey and 'up' track moved to the Heaven-on-Earth tune *Riverside* by Agnes Obel, and if there's one 'go outside this book and get this' instruction you have to follow, it's go and listen to this song, because it is so beautiful. It makes me want to cry and get on my knees and thank the universe for dropping me into this particular stream/ river of creativity today.

To get to share this with you; to get to do what I love, which is conveying the sometimes-wise-sometimes-potty stuff in my head to you. And for it to touch you, just as it all touches me; just as the art of this music is touching me now. Yes, for it all to touch you. Just the standing still here now can touch you – realizing what you've been missing, feeling a little bit sad for the time you've wasted not being in the stream, and feeling excited for yourself that you can now access more of this stuff in your life.

Wow, that's so bloody exciting… and it may not be all the time – crikey, it's very unlikely to be all the time, unless you're smoking something from dawn 'til dusk. But you

I do this practice in clubs as a two-hour 'F**k It Experience'.

can access this: you can feel better, you can actually start to FEEL, and you can start to do more of what you love.

And wow, Part II. The next song on the playlist is Pink Floyd's *Mother*, from the album *The Wall*, which saturated my aural space in the early 1980s. Again, it takes me right back to those times… this song really got me in touch with some unnameable sadness in me; some probably unknowable ancestral shadow that had something to do with the wars… there was a wall between me and the comprehension of that thing, but I could feel it, even if I couldn't understand it.

I have to share this playlist with you, don't I? But you see where this can take you? How are you doing?

Let that be your practice for a few days – hopefully for a few weeks, and possibly a few years. You can do it for as little as 10 minutes (adjusting the music timings accordingly). I usually do it for 20–30 minutes. In our live sessions on the retreats we can do it for more than an hour. And I do a full-on 'F**k It Experience' in clubs that lasts two hours.

This particular practice does you a lot of good. It's our way of doing 'spontaneous Qigong' and I talk a lot more about it in the 'Express It' chapter of my *F**k It Therapy* book. There, I concentrated on the healing effects of this practice. Hold on, given that you might well not have that book to hand, let me copy and paste a few good bits in…

Free Qigong (and you don't pay later)

One of the most powerful practices during a F**k It Retreat is officially referred to as Free (or Spontaneous) Qigong. It's usually only taught after a lot of Qigong practice. We often teach it on the first day. It's not dangerous, though it can look a bit potty from the outside. We introduce newbies to the wonderful healing art of Free Qigong by inviting them to ask themselves, 'What do I feel like doing?' Though that's not a way I've ever seen it taught.

The first time I came across Free Qigong was in the mid-90s, when I enrolled in a Qigong course with a great Chinese master, Simon Lau, in South Kensington in London. He taught Qigong very methodically, very slowly: teaching over weeks the philosophy behind it and how to simply stand and let the qi flow. He taught a basic form, too, but the emphasis was on standing.

I was there for around six weeks, but I had to skip several classes because I went off on a shoot for a TV commercial somewhere. When I returned, most of the people in the group seemed to have changed. We began the standing practice, just as I had learned and practised while I was away. I had my eyes closed and was really enjoying the sensation of the qi flowing in my body.

Then I heard banging coming from elsewhere in the room. I resisted the temptation to open my eyes and continued to stand. Then I heard other noises: someone was grunting, another person started to moan, and there was a louder banging, as if someone was stamping hard on the wooden floor.

I resolutely kept my eyes shut, and tried to keep my attention within my practice. But it was hard. The noises got louder and more varied. Over the course of the next 30 minutes, I heard someone howling like a wolf, another person moaning as if they'd had their pet kitten taken away from them – and then the sound of the pet kitten that had been taken away – and what sounded like someone beating their chest. I never went back.

A few years later, I was doing a Qigong course with another powerful Chinese Qigong master, Dr Bisong Guo. After a few weekends of practice, she too started to leave more space between the teaching and the formal set exercises. In one of those sessions, with nothing being said, nothing being done, just the space to sit or lie around and just be, I, again, was enjoying the peace and the feeling of qi flowing around my body.

Then, suddenly, there was a noise: the sound of a hand beating some part of the body… then a rhythmic guttural sound, like a Native American chanting by the fire. It was a shock, especially when I realized something. It was me! Me doing the beating! Me doing the chanting thing! I hadn't thought about doing it. I hadn't wanted to do it. But it had just happened – really naturally. And there was no stopping it. I seemed to be doing stuff and expressing stuff that I hadn't consciously thought needed doing or expressing.

And I loved it. Soon everyone was at it – or most of us, anyway. Others were asleep. Though I don't know how they slept through that racket. The racket was just like the one I'd heard a few years earlier, and had run a mile from. Only now, I was helping to make it. This time I really got it: when you relax enough and tune in enough and settle enough, eventually the qi starts to move and, if you fancy it, you can follow that movement.

Sometimes you feel like shaking, sometimes stretching, sometimes running around, sometimes shouting or howling, or sometimes sobbing. You don't decide to sob, the sobbing just happens. You don't decide to do the downward dog, the downward dog just happens. You open the door to it and that downward dog just bounces in to do its downward thing.

Free Qigong is VERY healing. You know it while it's happening, if you're aware of anything at all. When you let go and give in to whatever's going on there, you're unleashing whatever it is below (or above) all that's normally going on: whether it's the qi, or your instinct, or your higher self, or the Holy Spirit (those evangelical Christians get into some pretty freaky-looking stuff in the name of the Holy Spirit, including speaking in tongues).

When you let go, you naturally begin to Express It. Whatever it is that needs to be expressed. Well, it's not even that you express it: the expressing just kind of happens.

So, yes, I talked mainly about the healing effects of this 'practice' in *F**k It Therapy*. But the wider benefits of this practice are to train yourself to live spontaneously — real 'F**k It Living' — to train yourself naturally to Live By Doing What You Love.

You see, after you've done that practice for a while — maybe a couple of weeks — you no longer have to keep asking yourself the question 'What do I feel like doing?' Because you just naturally start to move with the flow and desire of things. Imagine starting to do that naturally in your life. I mean, it's a big enough transformation to be asking yourself, all the time, 'What do I feel like doing?', and then saying F**k It and doing it... But imagine if you just did it naturally.

Train yourself to live spontaneously — real 'F**k It Living'.

That's the essence of the 'going with the flow' idea of Taoism. It's one cool way to live. Gaia is very good at it. Just as she's always been very good at the natural 'follow-your-qi' practice. Here's another bit from *F**k It Therapy*, when I was writing about her —

Gaia and Qigong

Gaia has done Qigong for years, like me. And Gaia is particularly intuitive, trusting and spontaneous. Any of you who know her will regard that as an understatement. So Gaia was particularly into Qigong over the course of a couple of years.

She'd do hours of it a day. She'd get up in the middle of the night to do it (the qi varies at different times of the day and night). And she'd do Free Qigong outside in the early morning.

At the time we lived in a rented house on a hill, and around the house was a garden, and there were pretty steep drops on all sides. You probably wouldn't kill yourself if you fell down one of those drops, but it wouldn't be a pleasant journey. The whole area was like that: little flat bits, some tracks and roads, and steep fields and drops. Well, Gaia would start doing her Qigong – which would usually mean rolling around in the grass, or running around the garden at high speed – with her eyes closed.

She came in one morning – with bits of twig and grass in her hair, as usual – and told me about her 'practice' (clearly a ridiculous word for what she was doing). She had been running around the garden as usual, narrowly missing falling off the edges, and the qi had taken her off.

She just wanted to run. So she ran… and ran… and kept running. No, not like Forrest Gump, who ran for months. But she just ran – all the time with her eyes closed. Yes, indeed. Then she felt like stopping, so she did. Then she was guided to put her hand out, so she did. And, for the first time that morning, she opened her eyes. There in front of her, was a horse, sniffing her outstretched hand.

Now we wouldn't recommend doing that at home. But we do highly recommend doing this shaking and 'What do I feel like doing?' practice at home… then spreading it out into your life.

Pause. Have a cup of tea.

""""""""""""""""""""""""""""

.I was walking around the island of Gili Trawangan in Indonesia, looking for a place to see sea turtles, when I came across a diving club. Although I was terrified at the idea of diving, I said, 'F**k It, why not?'

I fell in love with that wonderful underwater world and with diving. A new passion was born. I said F**k It again and extended my stay three times. I now hold a PADI advanced open water certificate, and am off on my 14th dive this afternoon – whoop whoop!

BARBARA MARTENS – BELGIUM

""""""""""""""""""""""""""""

F**K IT, NO (SORRY)

Though I put myself down a bit earlier on (in the context of this spontaneous living idea), when I shared my rigid-non-blank-page-heavily scheduled-living with you, just in the process of writing this all down, and shaking with you as we've gone along, I've realized that I've incorporated the fundamentals of living spontaneously and saying F**k It to the rest rather successfully. Maybe I've done it so effectively and naturally that I don't even notice.

> *I've rather successfully incorporated the fundamentals of living spontaneously and saying F**k It.*

So here's me patting myself on the back. I fancy carrying on writing tonight, as there's an on-the-roll feel to this chapter. I've just pulled out of a dinner that I should be attending, but this is important for me to do – to follow this particular flow. And I'd honestly prefer you just to get on with the practice yourself, and then spread it out into your own life quite naturally. But I'll give you a few insights into how it starts to work.

It means saying 'no' quite a lot. Saying 'no' to what you're expected to do, by others or by yourself; saying 'no' to commitments you've made, and to ways of behaving that you and others have become accustomed to. 'No' becomes a beautiful, liberating word. Add 'F**k It' to it when you need to – i.e. 'F**k It, no' – and add 'sorry' to it where social niceties dictate, i.e. 'F**k It, no... sorry.'

'No' is a beautiful, liberating word. Add 'F**k It' to it when you need to.

It means saying, 'It doesn't matter so much' quite a lot, too. Because we're so full of our (usually adult) patterns and our (usually adult) cares and concerns, we have to tell ourselves constantly that 'It doesn't matter so much' and follow our own (spontaneous) path. If we go back to the practice, it's like being told to stand stiff and straight. But you want to move freely... so you say, 'Oh, that command doesn't matter so much: I must move, that's what I need.'

Add 'F**k It' to 'it doesn't matter so much' when you need to – 'F**k It, it really doesn't matter so much' – especially when the weight of what is mattering so much, but is holding you back, is feeling too heavy. It means travelling lightly and not taking things too seriously.

F**K IT, IT DOESN'T MATTER SO MUCH.

This F**k It Push Mantra: This is in the all-time top-three F**k It Mantras. Do not use it if you're averse to change, freedom and a good deal of letting go.

But you know that already, don't you? You see how I do it... I'm blessed that it happens naturally for me – probably with a hand from something I learned from my dad: the inability to let much conversation go without a joke and a laugh. The moment things are getting too serious, too earnest, too tight, or overbearing, I just see the silly side and want to laugh.

Don't hold on to anything too tightly – whether it's a job, or a thing (a car, house, etc.), or a person, or an idea of how you are or who you are, or how the world should be, or how others should be. Hold it all lightly. Hold it like a little bird in your hand: too loose and you let it go completely, too tight and you kill it. And I've seen too many dead little robins on my doorstep this past winter to like the idea of dead little birds.

❝❝❝❝❝❝❝❝❝❝❝❝❝❝❝❝❝❝❝❝❝❝

I said F**k It to my old office life – which was full of stress and worries – and started scuba diving; along the way, I met my future husband and I bought a boat in the south of Croatia. I've now started offering tours for tourists, who live on board my boat and experience the power of energy through water, wind and earth.
RAFFAELA HARTL – VIENNA, AUSTRIA

❞❞❞❞❞❞❞❞❞❞❞❞❞❞❞❞❞❞❞❞❞❞❞

By the way, if there's anyone out there who speaks 'cat', can you please tell all the cats that, yes, we really appreciate the *thought* behind those gifts of dead birds and mice and moles that you bring us, buuuutttt – and it's not a big thing – could you please expand your range of gift ideas? A nice bouquet of wild flowers, say, or a stone that reminds us of something else, like a small bird.

And, if it has to be 'food', can it be food that we like? I mean it's not personal, but we don't all have cat-like tastes. Ideally it would be something containing chocolate, if you could push yourself to procuring such a thing… Please, cats… after all, we do want to continue to get along as well as we do. In short, then: no more robin-red-breast-cute-but-dead-birds… please.

F**K IT, ALL THERE IS, IS HERE AND NOW.

*This F**k It Push Mantra: Enlightenment in nine words. Described in seven.*

Okay, folks, are we getting the hang of this Living By Doing What You Love/F**k It Living business? If you're struggling, this might help. Talking of cats: Be More Cat. Or, to circle back round to our original point: Be More Child.

Saying F**k It is key to being more child, because the child is naturally F**k It. The child's brain even operates at a different frequency: alpha (whereas an adult brain operates predominantly at beta frequency). When we really relax, our brains switch to alpha, with all that this means: we are, like children, more present, less inhibited, more open, less anxious and things seem less 'heavy' than usual.

*Be more cat.
Be more child.
And to get there,
be more F**k It.*

The alpha brain wave state is very F**k It – the child state is very F**k It. And, therefore, saying F**k It can take us back to that state. (This principle works with other aspects of the alpha brain wave state too: your breathing will deepen in that state, so breathing more deeply when in beta state will help switch you to alpha!). F**k It, then, is the bridge to the alpha-child state. So yes, be more cat. Be more child. And to get there, be more F**k It.

F**K IT, I'M FINE MAKING MISTAKES.

This F**k It Push Mantra: Maybe you'll enjoy the intentional 'mistake' of turning this mantra upside down. Maybe it will just annoy you. Well, I'm fine taking the risk, because I'm fine making some mistakes – it's the price of living on the hinterland of my (and everyone else's) comfort zone.

6

MAKING A LIVING BY
DOING WHAT YOU LOVE

'Success follows doing what you want to do.
There is no other way to be successful.'

MALCOLM S. FORBES – PUBLISHER OF *FORBES MAGAZINE*

If you're not already making a living by doing what you love (and let's assume you're not, given you've started reading this bit), I'd like to think (and say) that it will be easy. But, sorry, it's usually not. Sure, there'll be aspects of it that you find easy. It depends on your skill set – more on that later.

But the whole thing can be very daunting, and that's one reason why I've chunked it all down into steps: if you just follow these steps, one by one, you're going to get a significant way down the road to making a living from doing what you love.

But it takes something else, too. That something else has a F**k It quality and can thus be vocalized and utilized by saying F**k It when you need to. You need the F**k It to buckle down when things seems too daunting. You need the F**k It when other people are asking you what the hell you're doing. You need the F**k It when you get stuck somewhere and can't see your way out... you say F**k It and you persevere until you find that way out and through.

❝❝❝❝❝❝❝❝❝❝❝❝❝❝❝❝❝❝❝❝❝❝❝❝❝

I said F**k It to the horror, fear and shame that came when, through others' indiscretion, we went into financial meltdown – almost, but not quite, losing everything. It was a painful time, but once I let go of the internal mind babble I presented myself with the opportunity to retrain.

I'm now a registered psychotherapist, and I absolutely LOVE what I do. I live by the punk rock spirituality mantra of F**k It.

CHRIS MADDEN – YORKSHIRE, UK

❞❞❞❞❞❞❞❞❞❞❞❞❞❞❞❞❞❞❞❞❞❞❞❞❞

You need F**k It when you've done all the work and you launch your thing, whatever it is, to the world and the world then ignores it. You say F**k It when the money doesn't, at first, come in. F**k It can be about giving up and slowing down. And F**k It can be about getting moving and speeding up. Yang as opposed to yin F**k It. Well, in this part of the process of being able to Do What You Love, and earn a living from it, you're going to need plenty of the yang variety.

> *F**k It is the 'yes' or 'no' thing on steroids.*

It seems to me that life is often about what you say 'yes' to and what you say 'no' to. Well, F**k It is the 'yes' or 'no' thing on steroids.

This chapter is all about 'yes'. *Yes, I can actually earn cash from doing what I really love. Yes, I can do this, even though I've never done it before, and it feels so difficult. Yes, I will carry on, even though it's not working – I will persevere until it does.*

And F**k It is the injection of steroids into that 'yes'. F**k It is the slap on the back; it's the 'COME ON' of your coach; it's the rallying cry of Henry V at Agincourt to 'STIFFEN THE SINEWS, SUMMON UP THE BLOOD, IMITATE THE ACTION OF A TIGER.'

So, come on, F**k It: let's do this thing.

MAKING MONEY FROM DOING STUFF YOU REALLY LOVE

'Your work is going to fill a large part of your life, and the only way to be truly satisfied is to do what you believe is great work. And the only way to do great work is to love what you do. If you haven't found it yet, keep looking. Don't settle.'
STEVE JOBS

Right, think about this – how much time do you commit to the thing that makes you money? Do include travel time, preparation time, etc. in your total. Actually, if you sit moaning about your job to your husband/ wife/friend in the evenings or at weekends, include that time too.

What did you get to? Eight hours a day, 10 hours a day… more? Now take off the time you spend sleeping, and the time you spend doing non-work stuff that you really don't enjoy (like household chores), and what do you end up with?

That's your life, that is. Passing hour by hour, day by day, quarter by quarter. Until the sand in the egg timer runs through. Now, let's say you're lucky, and you get to spend a couple of hours a day *really* doing what you love – whether that's a hobby, or a sport, or sitting watching the TV with your family.

The thing is, if you want to expand the amount of time you spend on this planet doing something you actually like or even love, the biggest area of opportunity is during the time that you spend earning money. Usually, as well as keeping you and any loved ones sheltered, heated, watered and fed, you earn that money to spend on things you love, don't you?

It's a rational choice as much as anything. It's an easy(ish) win. It's the most obvious low-hanging fruit. Want to enjoy your life more? Then first address the biggest chunk of time that you spend *not* enjoying yourself – and that is, usually, the time you spend earning cash that you redistribute later.

" "

I said F**k It, made friends with my fears and set up a company doing what I've always wanted to do – making films. Now I wake up every day with a smile on my face because I know that day belongs to me and me alone.

ALEX GULLAND – LONDON, UK

" "

Incidentally, a recent Gallup survey indicated that 70 per cent of US workers hate their jobs. Oh, and don't now feel stupid because you too have wasted so much time in your life doing something that you don't really enjoy in the hope it will kind of be worth it (either at the weekend, or on that holiday, or – YIKES – once you retire).

No, don't feel stupid at all. Because the idea that we must knuckle down and do stuff that we don't enjoy is deep-rooted in our society. And the deep roots of this deep-rootedness are many and varied. For example, I was raised with an inherited Protestant work ethic – the notion that hard work was a good thing in itself, no matter the content of the work. But that was passed down to me by people who probably didn't have much choice about what they did for a living: 'It's the factory or the shop, lass – take ya pick.'

The idea runs deep. Our boys are constantly being told at school that they need to learn how to buckle down and do things that they don't like… that it's a prerequisite for a fulfilling life. Now this may well be a lame excuse for lame teaching methods, but it's what the teachers actually believe (and, as I think only about 10 per cent of the boys' teachers really enjoy their jobs, is that so surprising?).

Research, too, tells us that it's an understanding of 'deferred gratification' that leads to success in life. If you can learn to get your head down and do the things you don't want to do, and defer the pleasure of reward until later, you're more likely to be 'successful'. And by 'successful' I suspect they mean becoming lawyers and consultants and CEOs, rather than, say, librarians, nurses, delivery drivers, shopkeepers, and so on.

Imagine Doing What You Love and making a living from it. Wow!

No, don't feel stupid if you've been wasting so much time doing something that you don't really enjoy – this is how the majority of us live. But imagine spending all those hours that you currently spend doing something related to earning money, doing what you love. Just imagine it. Doing what you love, and making a living from it. Wow!

Incidentally, Leone, one of our boys, asked me this morning what I was doing. 'Writing about how to make a living from doing what you love.' I replied. 'Oh,' he said.

'Do you know what that means – to make a living?' I added.

'Si, farsi una vita,' he replied. (Remember, we're in Italy, and Leone's main language is Italian, even though he speaks English very well.) Translated back into English (we're going round and round here, aren't we?) that means 'Yes, to make yourself a life.' And there we have it – maybe by starting to make a living from doing what you love, you could be making yourself a life… a new life. Thank you, Leone, for that insight.

Do you really want to make a living from doing what you love?

Now I know that seems like a funny question, but it's worth asking, and it's worth checking it out at this stage ('this stage' being just before you dive in and start to work out ways to make some cash from doing the stuff you love).

When I think of this question, I think of my brother-in-law, Saul. For as long as I've known him he's had two primary passions: photography and cars. And just as I wrote that I saw another rather obvious path he could have chosen – taking photographs of cars. Anyway, he's never made his living from either photography or cars.

Over the years, I've suggested ways in which he *could* do that (it's always been a passion of mine, this 'doing what you love as much as you can' thing). But his answer has always been the same – *I don't want to.*

'What do you mean, you don't want to?' I always ask. 'You're doing a job you don't like – spending all those hours working and travelling back and forth to work – just to earn money to spend on cars and cameras so you can do something you *do* like at the weekends. You really don't want to?'

'No.' That's usually what he'd say: just 'no'. So I'd shut up. But on one occasion he explained his reasoning to me: taking photographs is a pleasure for him precisely because it's NOT work. If he suddenly had to earn money from it, it would become work, and therefore something he wouldn't enjoy.

I didn't really get this, but he explained that work is something you just do – you don't *have* to enjoy it. He knew that if he took photos for a living, he wouldn't enjoy it. Period (as he might have said if he'd been brought up in North America rather than Northern England).

Now, there could be logical reasons for this thinking – maybe the inherent stress in having to forge a living from photography, in a market that's likely crowded and difficult, might start to 'infect' the very act of taking photos. But I think it was simpler than this for Saul. Work is Work. Leisure is Pleasure. Work is Not Pleasure. Leisure is Not Work. There's an oil-and-water-don't-mix simplicity to this, isn't there?

But it's a view that I reject. I often 'fry' eggs in water with a few drops of oil in it. The oil does (sufficiently) mix in with the water, and what you get is something healthier (than an egg fried just in oil) and tastier (than an egg cooked just in water).

I think trying to make a living from doing what you love can be both healthier and tastier. I've never 'ruined' anything that I loved by trying to make a living from it. The opposite, actually, as it enhances my experience of making music to think that people might enjoy what I produce and give me a few notes for the pleasure, too.

Sure, what *can* happen on this road to making a living from doing what you love is that you end up not doing what you love (through the peculiar nature of the process); or what you love simply moves on. We'll cover that later, but for now, check that you're not in the Saul camp, where you're adamant that you can't mix something you love with 'work'.

I make a (good) living from doing what I love

I say this because I hope that you want to learn these skills from someone who actually knows what he's talking about. And you'll know by this stage in the book that I know how to do what I love, and how to refine it. You've seen my 'Do What You Love (or not) autobiography' after all, at the beginning of this book.

But do I really know how to make a (good) living from this? Yes, and I always have done. Well, I have to say, my philosophy used to be a little different from what it is today. When I was in my 20s, this was what I thought – *I feel free when I do what I love, and if I do what I love, I'll be rewarded for it.*

It was a kind of 'F**k It, the money will come' philosophy. Which is (partly) correct. And it's very healthy. I didn't think about, or worry about, money (by the way, this is pre-family, pre-mortgage, pre-pension thinking!). By doing what I loved, and being good at it, I was offered great jobs and was rewarded well for it. But could I have become really wealthy on that? Probably not.

F**K IT, THE MONEY WILL COME.

*This F**k It Push Mantra: It will. Especially if you say this mantra enough times. It works magnetically – mysteriously, but certainly magnetically.*

In my 30s I had an additional thought – *I'll feel really free when I don't have to do anything for money any more.* Notice the change in tense there: I went from the present (*I feel free when…*') to the future (*I'll feel free when…*) – i.e. delayed gratification.

It worked, though: my focus on creating financial freedom by creating passive incomes that would support me without my having to do anything, created riches that I couldn't have imagined from the desk of the job I had in my 20s. We will talk more about 'passive' incomes in this chapter. So, it worked for creating the money. I can't say I was particularly doing what I loved, but that's 'delayed gratification' for you.

I'm now in my 40s. What do I think now? Well, my earlier thought – 'Do What You Love and the money will come' – can be true, though it depends on the industry you're in… and it's usually best to be employed by someone. The focus on wealth creation I had in my 30s really can work, though it depends on many things – and it's usually best if you're your own boss. But it often entails delaying your gratification.

F**K IT, DO THE FIGURES.

This F**k It Push Mantra: I need a F**k It to do the figures. Most of us do. But do them if you want to keep on track, make more money, and successfully make a living from doing what you love. Boring boring, but ultimately rewarding rewarding.

So now, I try to do what I love, but with one eye on the books, too (I mean financial 'books' here, though clearly these books that I write help with those kind of books too). I've seen that, though we might earn well if we simply love our work, we earn more if we keep one eye on the books.

This, now I think about it, is a simple synthesis of the view I had in my 20s and the view I had in my 30s. And it works: I'm getting to love what I do as much as I did in my 20s – with all the accompanying excitement – but with the financial security of my 30s.

Do your duty (to God and to the Queen)

I'm not really talking about doing your duty to God or the
Queen here, but I couldn't help adding that bit in brackets:
it's the promise we had to recite at Scouts, so I can't talk
about 'doing your duty' without hearing that in my head.
And anyway, I'm not sure what my duty would be, to God
or the Queen.

If either of them actually exist, that is – yes, I have almost
as much doubt about the existence of the Queen as I do
God. She's obviously made up: played either by a series of
actresses, or by a robot. Actually, the actress thing makes the
Helen-Mirren-playing-the-Queen-thing very meta, doesn't it?

But anyway, with all this talk of doing what we love, there's a
danger that we don't pay attention to some of our duties. I
realize that doesn't sound very F**k It, and I also know that
if there's one thing that's got you into the mess you're in
(i.e. not doing what you love), it's the long list of duties that
you have.

Don't throw the baby out with the bath water, though,
because there are some duties that we do, of course, have to
continue with. Such as the duty of feeding our kids, or paying
the bills, or doing the books – and submitting a truthful
declaration of the contents of aforementioned books.

Now I'm hoping that your 'duties' will reduce over time.
Either because you don't have to do them (because you
decide you don't have to, or because someone else is doing
them), or because you start to like them, so they're no longer
'duties' but part of what you love. Funny that, isn't it? As soon

as you start to love a duty, it stops being a duty. It's like an annoying and rather scary ghost that, as soon as you decide to love it, vanishes forever. (Not that I believe in ghosts. Though I place the probability of their existence marginally above that of the Queen.)

There are many duties that, for a variety of reasons, will support you in being able to Do What You Love. And doing the books is the obvious one there. So please, when you need to, do your duty – with as much grace as you can muster.

Two words that should be dropped from the dictionary

Words usually drop out of a dictionary because they're no longer being used (just as words are added to a dictionary because they are being used). But I was thinking rather playfully, when I wrote that heading – I was thinking that we should deliberately lose two words in particular (the ones coming soon to a page near you), because their use is holding us back. (That's a very Orwellian, *1984*-like thought, though: as good as my intentions are, we can't go around suggesting that we take words out of the English language, in order to 'help' people.)

So these are the two words (though, after all that, one of them is pushing the definition of 'word' as it's actually an abbreviation). Anyway, here goes:

* Career.
* CV (curriculum vitae).

By the late 20th century, the idea of having a 'job for life' had started to seem old-fashioned, and instead having a 'career' became the thing. Today, though, the whole 'career' thing is starting to feel so 20th century. A 'career' is when you stay in the same line of work, and (hopefully) work your way up the career 'ladder'. How your 'career' progresses will have certain rules: about qualifications, about the posts that you hold, about the papers that you write, or the awards that you win.

And whether you're 'successful' in said 'career' will have its rules too: do you have those letters after your name by the time you're 30? Do you make it to that role by the time you're 40? Well, many of us are saying F**k It to those rules and F**k It to careers.

*Many are saying F**k It to the rules around 'careers'.*

The problem with the idea of a career, is that it could hold you back when the time is right to move on (and out). If you ever hear someone say, 'Well, what about your career?', put in a suggestion to the dictionary-writing-people for the word to be dropped: then they won't be able to say it any more. Or instead, just ignore them.

F**K IT TO THE RULES.

*This F**k It Push Mantra: Rules are meant for breaking (except, of course, those that involve hurting people, or getting you into a courtroom – you know the rules we're talking about).*

Same with the curriculum vitae (CV). That idea is so old, the words used are Latin – and Latin has not been spoken for 1,000 years, except by people who have careers in teaching the language to people who don't want to learn it.

I have never written a CV, and I never will. Okay, I admit to the possibility of a strange circumstance in which I'll be obliged to offer up my CV. In which case, I'll write it in Latin. That'll be my defiant, last-gasp way of saying F**k It – *Futuo id*.

If someone asks, 'Well, what about your CV?', say this to them – *Ponera tuus CV ubi sol non radiare!* – 'You can stick your CV where the sun don't shine!'

Being your own boss: it's brilliant

I do know what it's like to work for someone else. I did so between 1994 and 2001. For most of that time I had one main boss, and he was brilliant. He believed in me, and he gave me a lot of freedom to do my own thing (but with the right direction when I needed it). I build a grand statue to you now, Axel Chaldecott.

I had, I think, one of the best experiences of working for a company, but, since 2001, I've been my own boss – either freelancing or, since 2004, with my own company. And it is, I have to say, something else. You can't know it unless you do it. And, F**k It, I'll say it – it's BRILLIANT.

Here's why:

* **You can work the hours you want.** I can, if I wish, any day of the week, spend the morning in bed, have a leisurely lunch, and then go to the beach for the afternoon.

* **You're in control of your own destiny.** Gaia and I get to decide what we do with our business – whether to go for a new opportunity, or to concentrate on what we know; whether to go out and find new clients, or just work with our existing clients; whether to go for growth or to

downsize and work less. It's entirely down to us. So when we do well, I know quite a bit of that is down to us.

* **No one can tell you what to do.** We make our own decisions about everything. Sure, we have clients, guests, readers, partners in projects, and we listen to everyone… but no one can tell us what to do. And that's worth a lot.

* **With a small business you can spend a lot of time on your own.** No office politics, no competition, no distractions, no coffee-machine nonsense, no ridiculous office parties, no pointless presentations. Just no.

* **You get to do a wide range of jobs, and realize you *can* do them all.** This is something I didn't anticipate before I became my own boss. As a creative in an advertising agency, I was very strictly a creative in an advertising agency: I didn't have to research the market, or liaise with the clients, or do the accounts, or organize the photoshoots, or shoot the commercial, or fix meetings, or do the budgets for the business, or book the media, or hire people, or fire people, or talk to the City, or talk to the press…

Instead I had to sit around all day thinking up ideas for commercials. Everything else was done by other people. But since 2001, I've learned to do just about everything that a business needs in order to function: I make the tea, I work out the business strategy, I take bookings, I talk to the media, I do the accounts, I write the emails, the books, the website; I negotiate, I create contracts, I hire staff… And it's been amazing for me — as someone who just thought he was very good at coming up with ideas — to realize I can do all that stuff.

* **You get to reap the rewards.** When a business goes well, there can be some great rewards. Even in a small business, a moderate level of profits can make you a lot more money than you'd earn in salary in a similar business.

Being your own boss: it's shit

Sometimes, when I've been working too much, and am feeling the stress, I sit and dream about what it would be like to be working for someone else again: little responsibility, with a fixed amount of money hitting the bank account on a fixed day every month, tax paid. I sigh.

Because being your own boss really is something else. You can't know it unless you do it. And, F**k It, I'll say it – it's SHIT.

Here's why:

* **You can do the hours you want.** You can work all day, and then work in the evening (while your family are downstairs watching TV), and then work over the weekend (while everyone is at the beach). You can work during holidays, checking emails before your family get up. You can sneak away and work over Christmas and Easter, when people are doing the washing-up or snoozing.

   You can work on the bus, on the train and on the plane. You can work while you're waiting for someone. You can work while you're talking to someone about something else (isn't it funny how the most ordinary conversation can ignite great business ideas?). And you will. It's all down to you. There's always something to do: the list never gets shorter, and the opportunities never get fully grabbed.

* **You're in control of your own destiny.** And don't you know it? It's all down to you. You're responsible for it all working, and bringing in enough money to pay your mortgage and look after your family. You're responsible for your staff's mortgages and families, too. Every decision you make has an impact on other people. And it's all down to you.

  You are split between sustaining the business you have, trying to keep it sharp, and breaking out and finding new opportunities. You're always split: fire-fighting, then finding new business; fighting your battle on more than one front. With control comes responsibility. And don't you feel it – right there on your aching shoulders?

* **No one can tell you what to do.** Though sometimes wouldn't it be great to be told what to do next – for someone just to say, 'Okay, if you're going to make more profits this year, what you need to do is…'. Sure, there are coaches aplenty, and they can do that, but it's not the same as your boss, or your client, just telling you what to do. In that case, there's a not-so-subtle shift in responsibility, as you get on and just do your job – the weight on them, the hours on you. And, wow, wouldn't it be nice to just do some hours sometimes, and be paid for them?

* **With a small business you can spend a lot of time on your own.** Gaia and I met in an advertising agency that contained the smartest, funniest, most creative, radical bunch of people that are likely to be collected together anyway near me for a while to come. In one day, I'd talk to maybe 40 people. I'd have inspiring conversations, learn

new ideas, get recommendations for books and music, challenge people, be challenged by people. Now on an office day, it's me and the screen. It's a pop down to the kitchen to get a biscuit. It's problem-solving with Gaia. And many days are office days.

* **You get to do a wide range of jobs, and realize you can do them all.** Oh yeah, Jack of all trades becomes the problem here. And time: there's never enough time to get something done properly if you've spread yourself too thin. Sure, you can hire people, and work with agencies and freelancers (we'll talk about that), but there's something about being your own boss that means it's usually best to know how to do it all anyway. I think it's about responsibility again.

  Boy, am I good at a lot of things now? But, hey, look at how excellent I am at a few things (like music) – shouldn't I be devoting most of my precious time to those things? That's what happens when you're employed, or you have an agent, or a publisher or a record label to do the rest of the stuff. Or at least it used to be like that. In most creative areas today, it's now a condition that you do more stuff yourself, especially in the areas of marketing and publicity, even when you have a label or a publisher or an agent. So get used to the name, Jack.

* **You get to reap the rewards.** Yes you do. And you get to suffer when things aren't so good. When you're your own boss, you're unprotected from the winds of change, and fortune. When it's good, it can be very good, and when it's bad, it can be horrid. Like an emerging market, it can go really well or really badly.

There's something about the nature of a small business that means it doesn't take much to swing it. You could argue that it's always possible to do well, whatever the market and the context. But you have to be very agile to react to a crashing market. If your thing is tea and everyone gets into coffee, it might take you a while to realize and then adapt or move on. Make hay while the sun shines, but do make sure you're happy to eat hay when it clouds over.

So there you go: everything that can be brilliant about being your own boss, can also be totally shit. That said, you can't stop those who want to go it alone. Even when they know what it's really like. You couldn't stop me. And I wouldn't go back.

❝❝❝❝❝❝❝❝❝❝❝❝❝❝❝❝❝❝❝❝❝❝❝❝❝

I said F**k It to the pressures/responsibilities of running a business and over-working myself. One afternoon I decided to close my business, leave my part-time job as a lecturer and enroll onto a PhD in music composition.

I now teach music part-time and spend the rest of my time writing music. This year I'll publish my sixth book. Saying F**k It could be seen as risky but it has actually given me the freedom to pursue my dreams!

HELEN MADDEN – YORKSHIRE, UK

❞❞❞❞❞❞❞❞❞❞❞❞❞❞❞❞❞❞❞❞❞❞❞❞❞

Why it's a brilliant time to quit the 9–5

We know lots of people who have read one of the F**k It books, or come on a F**k It Retreat here in Italy, and then said F**k It, and quit their 9–5 job. Sometimes, they know what they're going to do, other times they don't. Some go travelling, others set up their own businesses. What's certain is that there's never been a better time to do your own thing, and be your own boss.

And this is mainly down to technology. If the technology of the Industrial Revolution took us out of our cottages in the 18th century and dragged us into the drudgery of the factory and the world of mass production, then technology

> *Lots of people have said F**k It, and quit their 9–5 job.*

is this time setting us free, allowing us to move back into our cottages and create micro-worlds online.

I'm not just talking about jobs that are based online (such as an online shop): most areas of the market are being revolutionized by technology in one form or another. Whatever you have to offer – whether it's your own skills, or a product that you want to make or an idea that you want to make happen or a book that you want to write – it's easier now with technology. Mainly because you can access more people more easily and more cheaply than ever before, and make your offering to them. It really is a brilliant time to say F**k It, quit the 9–5 and do your own thing.

F**K IT, I'M OFF.

This F**k It Push Mantra: Short and to the point. This keeps you on that impulse.

Why it's a shit time to quit the 9–5

Not just yet though. It's not easy, developing ideas for how to Do What You Love and get paid for it, when you're in a blind panic about paying your bills.

It really is a brilliant time in history to say F**k It and quit the 9–5 and do your own thing. The global timing is good, in other words. You just need to choose your local timing very carefully. And it's usually best not to walk out of a secure job, and straight into the wilds of the market. That's not what we recommend. There will be a time – just not now. Because you have two hands, not just one.

You have two hands, so use them

You can take this literally if you want – if you use your hands for your work, you could actually think about using both of them. For example, if you're an artist, then using your non-dominant hand might create some interesting results. If you're a machinist, then maybe stick to what you know: we don't want any accidents. If you're a porn star, use the other hand occasionally for whatever you use your hands for.

But this is not really about literally using your hands. Think of it as a guiding metaphor for how you can approach Making A Living From Doing What You Love. First: that you have other passions, skills and abilities that you're probably not using, and discovering those will help you in developing an idea that you can make money from.

Also, it serves as a great metaphor for how to develop these ideas without leaving your current job. Imagine that you have one hand continuing to do the work that you're paid for, and the other (redundant) hand starting to stretch its fingers and consider what to do with itself.

Keep both hands active. You can then allow the dominant hand (your current work self) to ease off a little bit, as the non-dominant hand begins to work. That could mean, for example, that you look at going part-time in your current job, which would allow you to spend more time on these new activities. Going part-time is a great stepping stone to going it alone – though you may well find that you like it that way, and remain part-time.

That might well give you the 'best of both worlds' that I was exploring above, in the section about how being your own boss can be both 'brilliant' and 'shit'. Or it could mean that, if you're already working for yourself but want to branch out, creating another income stream takes the pressure off your existing line of (less loved) work.

So, with your non-dominant hand now awake and ready, what could you use it for?

F**K IT, I CAN MAKE THIS WORK.

This F**k It Push Mantra: You can. Keep telling yourself. And don't give up.

TURNING WHAT YOU LOVE INTO AN IDEA (THAT COULD EARN MONEY)

So it's time, if you're ready, to come up with an idea or two, or 10, for how to turn what you love into an actual idea that could earn you some money. I say 'if you're ready', but maybe you'll never feel ready for this. Maybe it scares you to death – in which case, F**k It, just get on with it.

Ideas, ideas, ideas (times 10)

Just get started. Don't worry about the quality of your ideas – you can judge them and test them later. This stage is just about ideas. In fact, I'd begin by aiming to get a certain number of ideas. Quality is irrelevant and quantity is everything. Start with 10 if you want

— get to 10 ideas as quickly as you can. Or 100 ideas, if you're particularly prolific.

Ideas are actually my area of expertise, so I come up with too many; that's one of my challenges, actually. But coming up with just a few ideas might push you, so don't judge: loosen up, and go for it. And, just so you know, this number thing really works — it's what I've always done to shut up the critic in my head.

F**k It, just get on with it.

In my first job, *on* my first job, we were given a brief to write a poster for Sky, to advertise a new TV soap opera called *Melrose Place* that was hitting the screens of the UK. Some of the agency's creatives would take half a dozen ads in to the creative director (the great John Hegarty, actually). But my creative partner and I decided to write 100 ads, then take them *all* into the creative director.

He looked at this huge pile of paper and then dropped it onto the floor. Then he leaned over and started separating the ads into two piles (we didn't know which pile was which). He then took one of those two piles and separated it into two further piles, one of which was much smaller than the other. The smaller pile contained four or five ads. He then laid those out on the floor, looked at them for a couple of minutes and then pointed at one with his foot: 'That one,' he said, and then turned away from us to get on with something else.

'That one' had a headline saying 'Eat More Beef' above the array of hunky actors that constituted the cast of *Melrose Place*. And 'that one' was soon presented, approved, shot, set and printed to create huge billboard posters that were pasted up around London and across the UK. One of which I stood under, late at night on a London street, saying, quietly: 'I did that, I did.'

Quantity not quality really works, then, to get you moving. You're effectively saying, 'F**k It to the quality' (for now). It really works to put your mind at rest, and when your mind is at rest, it is more creative.

It's when I'm tapping away like this, completely relaxed and not overly worried about the 'quality' aspect – not just yet – that the peculiar ideas just pop up. The silly things, the funny things, the stories, the sideways observations: they all come

*You're effectively saying 'F**k It to the quality' (for now).*

when I'm in that state. When you're relaxed it lets the fairies in. And I like fairies. Even in a chapter as practical as this one, I want to let the fairies in occasionally. If you don't like the fairies – if you prefer fairy-free, pragmatic text – sorry. For you. F**k It. It's me.

F**K IT, WHO CARES HOW GOOD THIS IS?

*This F**k It Push Mantra: This opens the door to huge creativity. Go wild. Make a mess. And do the cleaning up later (or have someone else do it).*

Now, I'm going to throw in suggestions that will feed your production of ideas. Stay loose, stay productive. Quantity not quality, remember.

Create a sheet listing what you love doing

If you used a notebook for the previous exercises, or tapped them into your tablet, it may well be worth transferring your lists of the things you really love to a large sheet of paper (I like to use A2-sized card). Then just look at them, and see what ideas they generate. F**k It, this doesn't necessarily have to be difficult.

Maybe you have 'I LOVE EATING CHINESE TAKEAWAYS' next to 'I LOVE MY PART-TIME JOB SELLING AD SPACE', and you realize

F**k It, this doesn't necessarily have to be difficult.

that the white cards of a Chinese takeaway carton could actually be used as a very interesting new piece of advertising space. That's an IDEA that could make you some money.

Create a sheet listing what you're really good at

So in this book, and in these exercises, we're concentrating on what you really love. But we shouldn't ignore what you're really *good* at, should we? So grab another big sheet of paper and get scribbling down what you're really good at (include the stuff that you don't particularly like, too, as there may well be a way of twisting it).

Now look at both these sheets (i.e. what you love, and what you're good at) and see if anything pops up. For example, you might be really good at using spreadsheets in your current role as an auditor in an accountancy firm, but what you really love doing is creating those little embroideries that say things like 'Home Sweet Home' – the ones that have inspired the design of our F**k It Push Mantras.

So you go to a client and offer to turn her rather healthy spreadsheet-generated quarterly figures line graph into an embroidery that she can display in the foyer of her company. She loves it. You get a job (on the side). That's using both your hands.

Incidentally, while we rest momentarily on the leaf of 'what you're good at', as well as 'what you love', a logical person would realize that a productive way to move forwards would be to create a Venn diagram from these two subjects – with 'what you're good at' as one circle, and 'what you love' as the other, overlapping, circle, and then take whatever is in the overlapping area and concentrate on that to generate your ideas.

Which you can do. We've even created an example here, so you can see how.

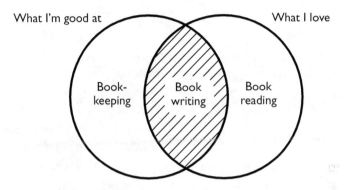

This is a Venn diagram, and a good one at that.

But, for me, competence in something is such a difficult area to judge – especially when you're judging it yourself. For example, can I sing? What did people say about Bob Dylan when he first started singing? Or Lou Reed? I bet many people thought they couldn't sing. That they weren't competent at it. Competence, like many things, can be a fashion.

F**K IT, WHO CARES HOW GOOD I AM?

This F**k It Push Mantra: If you're doing what you love, who cares how good you are – ignore the world's standards, listen only to your own.

And I'm not, by the way, suggesting that if you heard me singing, I would dismiss your view as out of fashion. I do not sing like Bob

Dylan or Lou Reed. But that didn't stop me from singing in front of 300 people three years ago. It didn't stop me from singing on the first song I produced, *Only Love* (if you want to hear that, just go to our website, www.thefuckitlife.com/dowhatyoulove – and if you don't like it, my, you're *so* not in fashion, man). For now, you can, if you want, say as much of a F**k It to competence as you have to quality.

Create an obvious idea

Don't miss the obvious idea or ideas. Don't miss the earliest ideas. The earliest and most obvious ideas are often the best. And they won't necessarily be obvious to other people either. Once you had your 'I'm good at spreadsheets' line sitting next to your 'I love doing embroideries' line, the IDEA was so obvious. Assume your idea is staring you in the face, right now.

Say as much of a F**k It to competence as you have to quality.

Create an unobvious idea

Most successes are things that stand out, and to stand out you need to be different, which usually means there has to be something somewhat dissonant about what you create: something that clashes with what people think, or might expect.

Clearly, our culture is in the accelerated competitive process of creating difference in every area. So we're bombarded by thousands of bits of information every day. To stand out from that cacophony of information, there needs to be a point of difference.

Putting two or more things together from your lists is a relatively easy way to do this. Especially when they're two or more dissonant things. I often do this, consciously or unconsciously: my first book, *F**k It: The Ultimate Spiritual Way*, was (and is) clearly very different in its market, and as a result, it stands out.

Now there wasn't such a step-by-step process in creating that book as there is here, but it arose from mixing my two sides: my rather serious, earnest, spiritual-searching side, and my irreverent, light-hearted, who-gives-a-shit side.

The title (and the book itself) creates an inherent juxtaposition, even an oxymoron, that is, yes, attention-seeking (and finding). But because it came from my truth, it also rings a bell with so many people – we're all a mix of sides. I'm inherently a living oxymoron, and you are too, most probably – if you don't mind me saying so.

So, have a go: start banging two things together that wouldn't normally go. I had a strange image there as I wrote that, which I'll share with you – it was of Ken banging Barbie. Now clearly that wouldn't normally happen (as Ken is obviously gay). You know, rough and hunky Action Man banging Barbie would have been more appropriate; or even Barbie on Barbie. But Ken on Barbie is somehow WRONG, and that's what makes it an enduring thought. (Note to editor: Can we please get a shot of a really well-dressed and coiffured Ken, banging Barbie over a miniature designer table? Editor: No.)

“““““““““““““““““““““

Three years after qualifying as a hypnotherapist, I was still dithering about setting up in business. It made sense to do it, but something was missing. I said F**k It and started teaching meditation and mindfulness instead. I love it!

LIZ SMALLEY – NEAR LEICESTER, UK

”””””””””””””””””””””””””

Create something to fill a gap

While the market you're in, or interested in being in – from guitar lessons to baby products and from web design to day-trading advice – might look busy and oversupplied to you, there will be gaps everywhere. If you find a gap, you make money. F**k It, it can be that easy.

The easiest way to find these gaps is to go from personal experience: what would you like to see that isn't there already? Let's take a random area for me as an example. Errmmm… clothing. I would love a jacket that has an inbuilt heating system; I would like gloves that feature a beeper system, so I can track them down when I lose them; I would like socks featuring unique symbols, so I can match them after a wash; I would like… Oh, and I could go on, believe me, but you get the picture…

*Find a gap, make money: F**k It, it can be that easy.*

Or – and again this is from my personal experience – explore something that's already out there, but is provided badly. I start this with 'It drives me mad…' Off the top of my head, here goes:

* 'It drives me mad that shops and bars located near car parks never want to give you change for the parking machines.' (The shop or bar that did do this would get a huge increase in traffic… maybe there could be a chain of shops located near car parks called 'We'll Give You Change'. And the name is also a pun: they'll literally give you change to use in the car park, but they'll also sell whatever stuff they sell at great prices, so they'll end up giving you change when you buy something from them… actually, we could go triple-pun here, and the great-value stuff that they sell could help change your life too.

* 'It drives me mad that I can never find a clean colander in which to drain my pasta.' (So, what about a saucepan with a panel in the bottom that has holes on the reverse, allowing the water to drain into the sink? A saucepan/colander in one.)

* 'It drives me mad, getting sales calls from utility companies all day, asking me if I want to switch suppliers.' (What about a phone with a car horn-like device built into it that you could just hit when you get such a call – blasting the ears of the offending time-waster? A kind of aural pepper spray, to be used against marketing muggers.)

Create something that's of real use to others

Being paid for doing something is just an exchange of 'value': when you have a value to someone, they express their appreciation for that by exchanging what you have of value to them (the service, product, skill, etc.) with what they have of value to you. This usually takes the form of the 'I Owe You' system of 'currency' that we use, so you can then take your IOU note and exchange it for something you value, like a new TV.

So what do you have, or what could you create, that's of real use to others? Maybe you have a skill that everyone comes to you for (you can fix remote controls), or you've invented something strange but useful (you can control your kids remotely from your office with a video 'baby' monitor – 'Put that down, Billy, I saw you.').

This question also gets us closer to the market-testing questions coming up in the next section: don't just offer, and produce and invent, in the hope that someone will buy it – instead, ask: 'What do people really need?'

Create something that would be easy to make money from

How could you make some extra cash, EASILY? Just think about it.

My sister and her husband (the aforementioned Saul) now have a business called 'Soul Trading' that pretty much started like that. Short of cash, they asked themselves that question – 'How can we easily and quickly make some cash?' They realized that they had bits around their house that they weren't using, so they listed and sold them on eBay.

And, as they looked around on eBay, they saw that some of the things they owned, and wanted to sell, could fetch a rather nice price. It might have been a particular lens for a camera that was now so sought-after it could command a high price. It might have been a limited edition Levi's jacket that Saul had bought in the January sales.

The 'F**k It way' to make a living from doing what you love may be the 'easy way'.

And, particularly in the area of clothing, they realized that they could sell certain brands and items at a much higher price than they were buying them for in various factory outlets or sales. So that's how they make their living: they know where to go, and when to go, and who to talk to, to find the really great bargains. They then buy a good quantity of what they find and sell it at a profit on eBay.

And that all started – their whole business – with the question 'What would be easy?'

If I were ever strapped for cash, and asked myself that question, I'd probably decide to start teaching Tai Chi locally. Once I had started teaching, I'd then ask myself the question again. And then I'd probably create a little video course of me teaching Tai Chi (easy). And put it online (relatively easy).

How can you make some extra cash from doing what you love? What would be EASY? Because there might be no more 'F**k It way' for you to make a living from doing what you love than this EASY way.

F**K IT, IT CAN BE EASY.

*This F**k It Push Mantra: Especially if you think it can. This is like a water pistol of ease that you can spray liberally on everything in your path.*

Create something that twists what you already make money from

Maybe you don't need to make a huge leap. Maybe you don't have to create the big new idea. Maybe you don't have to invent anything. Maybe you could just adapt what you already do.

It could be about doing what you already do in a different way – for example, if you make a living from painting portraits in oils, maybe you could start creating them using stained glass instead. Or it could be about doing what you already do in a different context – for example, if you're a lawyer at a big bank, and it's not doing it for you, go find a job somewhere you'd love to work, like a charity.

Or it could be that you simply take exactly what you do, and you become a consultant, or a freelancer. I know many people who've left their jobs, then gone back to consult for the same company; they are pretty much doing the same job as before, but on their own terms. In this context, 'terms' means 'hours' (read: work more when you want) and 'money' (read: a lot more).

“““““““““““““““““““““““““““

I said F**k It to climbing the corporate ladder and went freelance instead. Some exciting things happened: I discovered my job was actually quite interesting (once you stripped out all the corporate bullshit); I had space to think about what I was really passionate about and I'm now setting up my own business on the side.

People have started telling me they've been inspired to make their own changes by seeing me go for it – which has been amazing.
Charlotte Evanson – London, UK

”””””””””””””””””””””””””””””

Create 'the' idea from your 10 (or 100)

So, you're (hopefully) creating a nice list there of some interesting, potentially money-earning, ideas. Is there one that really stands out? If so, F**k It, dump the rest and take your winner into the next stage.

If not, if you really like four or five of your ideas, keep them all; live with them for a while and take them into the next stage – after all, the idea is to make money from these ideas, so it's worth digging down into which ones really could make you some cash.

TURNING YOUR IDEA INTO A MONEY-EARNING VENTURE

'The secret of living is to find people who will pay you money to do what you would pay to do – if you had the money.'
Sarah Caldwell – opera conductor and founder of the Boston Opera Group

Go ticking boxes

So does your idea (or ideas) tick the right boxes for you? Incidentally, I love a tick box. I use them all over the place when

I'm planning what I need to do. When I'm hand-writing my to-do lists, I use little tick boxes next to the items. At the end of this 'Go ticking boxes' point, I'll go to my list of chapters and tick the tick box next to this one.

Create your own list of things that could be important (at this stage, I mean – you could add others later). Here are some ideas:

Am I sure this is what I'd love doing? ☑

Am I sufficiently good at it? ☐

Is there likely to be a market for it? ☐

Am I sufficiently different to others? ☐

Have I finished now? ☐

Go pain-seeking

We're simple creatures, we humans: we want pleasure and we want to avoid pain. And, in fact, much of what we regard as pleasure is related to something that reduces pain. Just take the pleasure of eating, for example, (if, indeed, you take any pleasure from eating): I eat a meal to eliminate the 'pain' of hunger. I might eat a chocolate bar to reduce the 'pain' of feeling a bit low (by enjoying the serotonin hit that follows).

I might eat, in general, to numb the very pain of existence: by literally filling up I numb what figuratively feels empty. Oh, cheery John. But just writing that has made me somewhat hungry. When's lunch? Ooh, another two hours' time: bummer.

So as most of us are on a perpetual trip to eliminate the pain, or reduce it, or avoid it in the first place, then it's worth starting to figure out how you can help people on this trip. How can you help people with their pain?

Remaining on the food and drink topic, then: big advertisers still use the most basic pain-reducing invitations to entice us to buy their products. Coca-Cola vending machines have one word emblazoned across them: THIRSTY? They're asking, 'Are you in pain? If so, we have just the thing for you'. Similarly, burger chains will ask if you're HUNGRY?

This is not sophisticated – it's animal. And, appropriately enough, the animal answer to your animal urge when you see that animal prompt of HUNGRY? might well be to eat a bit of an animal (cushioned by two bits of sugar-and-salt-enhanced-and-processed-wheat bun).

Adding 'F**k It' to 'Do What You Love' increases the pain-relieving effect.

So, go 'pain-seeking'. Ask yourself, what pain are you relieving with what you have to offer? Is there any way you can increase the pain-relieving effect by twisting, focusing, or exaggerating what you do? Just as I'm doing with you – here, now. I've written this book, *F**k It – Do What You Love*, to help relieve the pain you feel at spending your precious time on this planet Not Doing What You Love.

To increase the pain-relieving effect of this book I've added that F**k It. This is not just 'Come On. Do What You Love', it's a twisted version – 'F**k It – Do What You Love' – which undoubtedly increases the effect.

I also increase the pain-relieving effect by 'focusing' on the individual steps that you have to take in order to be able to Do What You Love. I'll also be 'exaggerating' my suggestions as to how you can Do

What You Love ('How to earn $1,000 a day doing what you love') to demonstrate that it's possible to relieve your pain in a big way.

Once you understand the pain that your offer is relieving, it can really help your process. You can play with this (sometimes rather cynically, if that's what floats your boat), by splitting your consumer's pain into smaller parts, and relieving them one by one. Or you can even AGGRAVATE their pain so you can then offer the even greater relief of your product or service.

I've just been watching the US TV series *Fargo*. Martin Freeman's character, Mr Nygard, is an insurance salesman and, at the beginning of the series, he's a pretty hopeless one at that. In one scene, he has a newly married couple in his office, as potential clients.

Clearly insurance is, fundamentally, a pain-reducing concept: if something bad happens, we'll step in and help (usually with money). In trying to sell them life insurance – i.e. 'If the worst thing happens to either of you, we'll help' – Mr Nygard uses the technique of 'aggravating' the pain of this scenario by suggesting we never know what tragedy might befall us at any time… and he describes a couple of awful things that could happen to the husband today. The couple go white with fear, mumble a few words, and leave.

I have never consciously used such pain-aggravating techniques, but I look back to the beginning of this chapter, which is talking about 'Making A Living By Doing What You Love', and see that I asked you to imagine how long each day you actually spend doing what you love: after doing all the work that you don't love, and the commuting that you don't love, and the chores that you don't love, and I wrote, *That's your life, that is. Passing hour by hour, day by day, quarter by quarter. Until the sand in the egg timer runs through.*

Shit. Sorry. But that's pain aggravation. Big-time. Maybe, normally, you're barely aware of the fact that you don't really spend that much time doing what you love. Hey-ho, that's life. 'Sorry, can't stop – must get off to work.'

'No, hold on, you: *really* think about how pitifully little time you spend doing what you love.'

'Oh, yes, good grief, you're right – how awful. I must do something about that. My life really is miserable, isn't it? Can you think of anything?'

'Well, yes I can, since you ask.'

The miserable cycle of misery-reducing marketing. I didn't mean to do it, honest, guvnor. But you see how it works? You could also see it in a rather less cynical way: we are all in pain and looking to reduce and relieve that pain, and any way you and I can find to help is one hell of a service to the world, isn't it?

If I manage to increase the amount of time you spend doing what you love, by your reading this book; if I 'up' your joy quotient by 10 per cent, just by writing these 70,000 words for you whilst sitting here quite happy myself (just a bit hungry, thinking that it's still quite a bit more than an hour 'til lunch), then that will add to the joy I feel simply in doing what I love.

How will I know, by the way? Because lots of you write to me: you always have and I hope you always will. And I always reply. Because thanking people for thanking me for what I do, especially when it's about doing more of what you love, is something I love.

Go niche pain-seeking

There's some big generic pain out there – 'I'm hungry' and 'I'm thirsty' – as we've seen, and that makes for a huge audience. Probably the biggest audience possible. It's a little like saying,'HUMAN? Well, we have just the thing for you: FOOD and DRINK.' So you get mass products (Coca-Cola and McDonald's), mass-produced for low-price mass-consumption – probably at mass cost to our mass health and sanity.

'Hungry?'

'Yes, I am, but I don't want to eat that crap.'

'But I'm everywhere, reminding you not just that you're hungry, but getting you to project into the eating experience by suggesting that you're LOVIN' IT, even before you've tasted it'.

'Fuck off.'

'Hungry?' Silence.

'Thirsty?' Grrrrrrrrrr.

Big audiences seem good. What could be better than offering something great that every frickin' human on the planet would appreciate? Well, one problem (to start off with): they cost a lot to get to. It costs a heck of a lot to get to EVERYONE. Sure, that's what most of us are used to with marketing and advertising – the mass broadcast message for the mass offering. That's why the broadcast space is full of generic offerings (we all need to eat and drink and to drive a car and to use a phone and to know what number to call if we injure ourselves at work!).

But do you know how much it costs to advertise on TV during a programme that's likely to be watched by a lot of people? A lot, okay? And I suspect that you're not going to be earning that kind of money any time soon. So you have to reduce the cost of getting to people. And that doesn't mean sticking with your generic audience, and buying just 30 words in the classified section of your local newspaper.

It means narrowing down *who* you're aiming at, and that's called finding a 'niche'. (In the UK we pronounce that as 'neesh' and in the USA they say 'nitch', like 'snitch', though I'm not sure our American friends would know what a 'snitch' is. And even if they did, maybe they'd call him/her a 'sneesh'.)

Don't just go for people who are 'thirsty' – go for people who are thirsty for something very particular. A few years ago, for example, Gaia and I created a brand of very expensive Chinese tea. Don't just go for people who are 'hungry' – go for people who are hungry for something very particular. Chocolate is still too big a market, so we had 'F**k It Chocolate' for those who want to eat chocolate, but feel they shouldn't, but finally say F**k It and do – and are happy to walk around with a chocolate bar with an f-bomb on it.

F**k It Chocolate was our niche in the 'I'm hungry' market.

So whether you create a magnet that draws in your audience, or you pay to go to them, you want to be in a niche, appealing to a niche. Don't just go for the overweight, go for Men Who Still Think They're Thin, or Women Post-Birth, or Chocolate Addicts, or Those More At Risk of Some Disease, or People Who Like Takeaways… or any other way you can split your audience of all the people on the planet who want to lose weight, into a smaller group.

If you can reduce the size of your target market to a niche, and offer something that really appeals to them, then getting your message to them has never been easier. Really. Let's say that, inspired by the Kevin Spacey character in the film *American Beauty*, who starts getting fit because he 'wants to look good naked', you create a line of diet products called 'Look Good Naked'. Now, that's an appealing idea for

ANYONE who is carrying some extra weight. But you know it would resonate even more with those who understand the reference.

So you go on Facebook and start to define the target audience for your advertising as 'someone who has said they like the film *American Beauty* (it's possible to do this). So we've gone from everyone on Facebook (broadcasting) to just those who know the film that your product was inspired by.

But, you say, there are going to be plenty of people who saw *American Beauty* who don't need to diet. You would, therefore, be wasting your money. Well, apart from the fact that those people are unlikely to click your ad, and would therefore not cost you anything, you're right – it's best to get to as niche a niche as you can.

So you add 'dieting' as an interest and you probably have your niche. Now you say (again), who'd put 'dieting' as an 'interest'. Well, maybe not that many people. Maybe only those who don't take themselves too seriously – who know that they're overweight, but are happy to make fun of themselves a little: to admit that as well as 'skiing' and 'hiking' and 'twerking', 'dieting' is a kind of cool and funny thing to put.

And did you see I wrote 'not that many people'? That's exactly what you're after: Not That Many People. But Not That Many People who are exactly Your Kind of People. And I suspect that if you really did have a line of diet products called 'Look Good Naked', then the relatively small group of people who a. understand your reference and have seen *American Beauty* and b. are light-hearted, self-deprecating and kind of cool are probably very much Your Kind of People.

And getting to Not That Many of Your Kind of People with an offering that's Very Much You (and grows out of what you love) is going to be much cheaper, more cost-effective and ultimately more PROFITABLE than anything else you try to do.

> **" "**
>
> I said F**k It. Loudly. I changed careers entirely, leaving the structured, corporate world of research to become an abstract colourist painter. It was a massive leap to make: learning from scratch again, and with the attached grey areas of change and self-employment.
>
> How has it been? Well, it feels very natural. It feels right. Why? Because it doesn't feel like work: I am simply spending my time doing what I love – and I don't use the word 'love' lightly here, either.
>
> MAHLIA AMATINA – READING, BERKSHIRE, UK
>
> **" "**

Go hook-seeking

So, let's say you've found the pain that you're going to relieve. And you've found the niche who are feeling that pain. Now, what hook around your idea or product or service will draw in that niche? You can imagine this as a fishing hook – what tasty bit of bait do you need to affix to the hook to get some bites?

Staying in the area of food and weight loss: let's say you're a man who's lost lots of weight, and you want to write a diet book for other men. You're aware that there's a whole group of men out there who know that they're now overweight, but don't really want to admit it – they even see a thinner self in the mirror when they look.

What's your hook? How about – 'Guys, Do You Still Think You're Thin?' That's an interesting idea – to still think you're thin, even though you're clearly not. It's also instantly niching your audience: a. men,

b. overweight but not massively so, and c. self-aware (even though you're playing with a lack of self-awareness in your suggestion, you're actually appealing to self-aware, self-curious men).

You could follow your question with some facts. For example: unlike women, who suffer from body dysmorphic disorder in the other direction (i.e. they think they're overweight when they're actually thin), 30 per cent of overweight-assessed men believe they are

F**k It, I'd buy a book called This is Not a Diet Book for Men.

within 'normal' weight range. You might conclude, too, that men who don't really want to face the fact that they're overweight wouldn't really want to go on a diet.

So your diet book for men could be called *This is Not a Diet Book for Men.* And you could design alternative covers for the book, too – so if you're reading it in a public place, it could become a book about tanks. Or climbing. Or sheds.

I'd read an ad that said, 'Do You Still Think You're Thin?', because I know that, in the mirror, I *do* see myself as thinner than I actually am. F**k It, I'd buy a book called *This is Not a Diet Book for Men.* And I'd select the 'tanks' cover, since you ask.

You see? In this case, an idea for a hook, automatically (or practically) gave us a great niche that would be cost-effective to get to AND it gave us an idea for the actual product.

Nice. ☑

Go medium-seeking

No, not that kind of medium – though a bit of psychic advantage in the game of getting ahead in the market might not do you any harm — this kind: what's the path between you, your thing and the niche market? Sure, you have a hook, but what kind of media are you looking at? Is this a word-of-mouth thing? Is it a networking thing? Is it traditional advertising?

How you provide your thing to the niche will clearly have an effect on the media you use to attract them to it. So if your idea is an online dating agency, then you'll probably be looking at a range of online marketing media as a strategy: through both social and natural searches and then paid-for messages in a variety of ways.

Well, that's the logical route anyway, but maybe thinking about what single people do, and where they go, would lead you to an unexpected media channel that you could therefore get cheaper. For example, maybe there's a singles bar that would allow you to do some form of promotion.

When we opened our vegetarian retreat centre 10 years ago we did market in the obvious places (yoga magazines, holistic magazines, etc.). But I had an idea, which I never actually executed, that would have worked very well, I'm sure. I researched a list of all the vegetarian restaurants in London and in other big cities.

I knew that to somehow get into these restaurants would get me to my niche — a vegetarian who has gone out of his or her way to find a healthy vegetarian restaurant is someone who's likely to consider a holiday in Italy that offers healthy vegetarian food and other healthy holistic activities.

But how do we persuade the restaurant owners to put out our leaflets or cards? Practically impossible, I'd say. So my idea was to print our logo on paper serviettes, with a message along the lines of: 'If you enjoyed this food, you'll love this holiday. The Hill That Breathes — retreats with delicious vegetarian Italian food.'

And then we'd send a couple of boxes of these to every restaurant on the list. This wouldn't be just a sample they could throw away: it would be enough that they'd never throw them away (such places are eco-aware, remember). And it would also be something they'd find really useful – a couple of thousand serviettes FOR FREE. They have to buy serviettes normally, so they'd save the money. They'd effectively say, 'F**k It, we might as well use them.'

The medium is what connects you and your thing to your niche market.

So what's the cost? A little bit of marketing for a nice-sounding retreat centre in Italy. Can't be bad. And to increase the attraction even more, we could have offered to feature their restaurant in a little *Guide to Veggie Restaurants* that we'd put out in our dining room.

The medium is what connects you and your thing to your niche market. Yes, you're looking at the cost of marketing (and nowadays that often means the 'pay per click' digital media are very interesting), but do think about what could be different, too. About how you could stand out. Not just with your offering, and your hook, but in the *way* that you offer it.

The best example of unexpected media use that I've ever seen was devised by our mates Jim and Chas at the British advertising agency HHCL, which we all worked for during the 1990s. They were involved in advertising a new flavour – blackcurrant – of the popular fizzy drink 'Tango'. In fact, they created as fine an example of broadcast TV advertising as you'll ever see.

The new drink was selling well, but there was some problem with production, so the company had to withdraw the product whilst they sorted it out. Once they were ready to relaunch the drink, they wanted to say to people: 'Blackcurrant Tango is back', in a prominent enough way to get shops and grocers to order lots in.

Jim and Chas's aim was far from prominent, but astonishingly effective. It so happened that a couple of weeks before the relaunch (and restocking) of the drink, the huge and famous five-day Glastonbury Festival took place. There you go – all your target market in the same place. Now most ad agencies would have advertised at the festival with posters, banners, even a stall selling just Blackcurrant Tango.

But, no… Jim and Chas's idea was to 'litter' the festival site with empty Blackcurrant Tango cans. So they got plenty of empty cans from the client, battered them up a bit (to make them look like litter) and then had a team drop them around the site, in areas where people were dropping litter.

The idea was that people would see the cans, and later ask in newsagents and grocers for a can of Blackcurrant Tango. And the shops would have to say, 'No, they're not in yet, though we'll have loads soon.' Genius. People got a thirst for something without being directly advertised to, and the grocers got their best possible incentive to stock lots of Blackcurrant Tango – people actually asking for it. And, of course, this hugely innovative 'media' use (which wasn't media use at all) got press, and got talked about (once people sussed what was actually happening).

Go pleasure-seeking

Yours, not theirs. Now some of your ideas should be coming together – like a puzzle finally taking shape – with your special idea, your irresistible hook, your interesting use of media, and your niche niche.

Now, check in with how much pleasure whatever this thing you're thinking of could give you. And as we dig deep into the nitty-gritty of how to make money from it, keep this pleasure-seeking thing in mind… because there may well be ways to make some easy money from something that really doesn't float your boat – and that's probably not a F**k It path you want to take.

For example, if your thing is floaty-boats, maybe you'd adore taking Chinese-imported-bog-standard inflatable dinghies and painting them with weird and wonderful designs based on what your customer wants; maybe Cynthia has a thing for mermaids, so you design a fabulous Cynthia-as-mermaid painting for her that adorns her new seafaring inflatable. And you have people locally that come to you, mainly through word of mouth.

*If it doesn't float your boat, it's probably not a F**k It path to take.*

The obvious next step is to create a website, and start to advertise online, and sell online. But the whole website-online thing makes you feel sick, as if you're in a boat on a stormy sea. So that's the last thing you should be doing. You should be looking – if making some money is the thing you're looking at doing – at non-online ideas to get more people to buy your dinghies.

And that focus (i.e. your own pleasure) may well lead you into very interesting areas (market-wise); maybe better than the more obvious areas that are making you feel very ill. So maybe you donate a few of your painted-dinghy creations (featuring some suitably funky youth-appealing designs) to the local swimming pool, to be used by school groups, with the agreement that you can advertise in the reception of the pool (with photos and your details: it's a watery environment so you're at least getting to a water niche there). Bingo.

You see, speaking as someone who's been working (commercially speaking) with ideas for a long, long time, I've seen that it's often being presented with obstacles — you don't have the money to advertise, or your advertising is banned, or the price of your materials goes up, or the exchange rate with your primary overseas market changes, etc. — that forces even more creative ideas out of you. Necessity is the mother of invention, after all (which makes me wonder, of course, who the father was… Was 'invention' spawned during yet another drunken one-night stand?).

F**K IT, I'M DOING THIS FOR ME AND NO ONE ELSE.

This F**k It Push Mantra: Good for you.

So, if you make one obstacle 'I must get pleasure from this', you're likely to find a way to make money still… and (extra bonus points) your idea and the way that you offer it might actually benefit from the bastard 'invention' you squeezed in order to bypass said obstacle.

Bonus points. ☑

Go small-step seeking

How can you, with the smallest number of steps possible, start to generate some money from this venture? Start now, start small, take baby steps: say F**k It and do SOMETHING. Start to get the word out, have a go: don't think that you have to have it all planned out and perfect to get going.

Right now, there's a boom in digital information products — e-books, e-courses, etc. — that are available at a variety of price points online. You could turn something you know a lot about into one of these information products, and sell it online. The advantage (over traditional publishing) is that you don't physically have to make anything. It's low cost, and you can upscale (more on that later) easily without incurring extra costs.

Start now, start small, take baby steps: say F**k It and do SOMETHING.

It can sound difficult. It can sound complicated. It may well sound daunting. But it's just about knowing what to do, and getting on with it. I've created many such digital products myself, and, at this very moment, someone will be buying one of them and transferring anything between €7 and €700 into our Paypal account.

I've created a free introduction to this world of digital information products — at the usual www.thefuckitlife.com/dowhatyoulove — if you want to find out more. I'll then offer you more juicy information for €7 (and then more information after that too, at a higher price). That's the way it can work. How meta is that?

F**K IT, I WILL DO THIS, ONE STEP AT A TIME.

This Push Mantra: Ooohhh, this one works in so many ways and in so many contexts. If you're struggling in any way, just take that one step at a time.

Go make some cash

Strap it together and do it. Give yourself a very short deadline and make it happen. Set yourself a reasonable financial target, too — say to make $500, or whatever that would be in your local currency. And of course, what you aim at, and what you think you could make, depends entirely on the market you're in, and what you're after.

❝❝❝❝❝❝❝❝❝❝❝❝❝❝❝❝❝❝❝❝❝❝❝❝❝

I said F**k It and bought a share in a racehorse. And then another; and then another. You'll now find me trackside, cheering them home.

KATIE WHARTON – HAMPSHIRE, UK

❞❞❞❞❞❞❞❞❞❞❞❞❞❞❞❞❞❞❞❞❞❞❞❞❞

The amount you can charge teenagers for that cracking idea that you have will be different to what you can charge banking executives for another idea. Clearly. So, yes, just bolt together what you've been working on so far, and F**k It, just get on with it.

For example, you've realized that you love wandering around Ikea of a Sunday, and buying stuff that needs constructing – you love taking it home, working it out and making it. Your friends, too, know that you love doing that, and they now ask you to construct the things they buy from Ikea. They then throw you a few notes, or treat you to dinner (and you usually have meatballs: Italian, not Swedish).

*Bolt together what you've been working on, and F**k It, just get on with it.*

And you realize you could earn some money doing this. So you know your niche (people who like Ikea stuff but don't like putting the Ikea stuff together: people like me actually), and you're starting to get some ideas about getting to them. You know what you want to charge. You *could* now start to plan big things – work out a great name for the venture, with a well-designed logo and look. You could put a website together, get business cards made, think of ads with your 'hook' and work out where to put them.

OR… You could just send an email to your mates, telling them that this is what you're going to be doing, and how you'll be charging for it. You could also outline what you'll give them if they recommend you to others. (Don't offer your services to them directly – there's nothing more likely to close someone off than making them feel obliged.) F**k It, get moving, suck it and see, and then see what's next.

The problem with planning things in huge detail is that it stops you from getting on with things… and a very detailed plan also excludes the possibility of change as the situation changes. And change it will. Get on with it, and save the planning until later.

Go plan

Oh, is it that time already? *Later?* So, yes, I know what I just said about planning, but let's say you got on with things, and you're rolling, and you want to move to the next stage. So, allowing for the vast, potentially infinite, possibilities that you beautiful readers have before you, you should now have:

* **An Idea for Your Thing** (something that you love – a product, service, book, shop, skill, teaching, blog, craft item – which will, somehow, reduce the pain, or increase the pleasure, for someone out there).

* **An Idea for Your Thing's Target** (a group of people – or even just one person – who are 'niche' enough that it doesn't cost too much to get to them, and whom you can easily imagine and get to know).

   *   **An Idea for Connecting Your Thing with Your Thing's Target** (this could, at this stage, simply be your 'hook'; or it could be the position you've chosen to put your thing – like a shop, or that dinghy, or where you'd want to advertise).

Start now to do the detailed planning work:

Do the money-planning side

I often start with budgets for a project. What do you want to earn in total in a year? How do you get to that – how many units do you have to sell, at what price, and how much does that give you for marketing?

Incidentally, it depends on your market, but you can try to get your marketing to 'self-fund' – i.e. you pay for all your marketing budget with the introductory, smaller items that you sell to your customers, and then make your profits on the larger items you sell later.

Imagine your target market more vividly

Create 'avatars' of your target market: think of the individuals in your market, and sketch them out:

   *   Who would be your ideal customer?

   *   What's their name, where do they live, are they single or in a relationship?

   *   What's the biggest pain in their lives? How would they feel if they could have help with this?

   *   What is it about your offering that helps to relieve their pain in some way? How much would they be willing to spend to relieve that pain?

Sketch your avatars out in (huge if you want) detail. Blimey, write a book about them if you want. The more you get to know them, the more likely you are to create a real offering that appeals to real people. Because your avatars, though invented by you, will be made up of real bits of you and real bits of other people in your life, and will constitute a very specific 'everyman' (I'm not a moron, I know my oxymorons, remember) that you then go on to – and this is very peculiar – manifest in the real world.

Yes, imagine your customer, create your offering, and then go ahead and manifest hundreds or thousands of identikit customers like magic.

The Industrial Revolution began as people realized we could mass-produce, as if by magic, very similar things, and then go on to sell them to the masses. The current digitally enabled revolution means that we can produce as if by magic similar consumers, and then sell them masses of what they want.

Do everything you can to make your offering brilliant

Put everything you have into it. Make it of a higher quality than the others. Add more to your offering than other people would. Pay attention to the tiniest detail. Say, 'F**k It, I will make this BRILLIANT.' The more brilliant you make it, the more valuable it will be to people. And the more valuable it is to them, the more they will be willing to pay for it (in economics, 'price' is defined as 'what people are willing to pay', and the more value they see, to them, in what you're offering, the more they will be willing to pay).

Chunk every part of the process, then add timings

Work backwards if you want: when do you want to launch your offering? And what do you have to do to get there? Chunk it down into smaller and smaller parts and tasks, and then put timings on everything. Or work forwards – assess how long each step will take you, then create a realistic launch date based on that. I generally work backwards. There's nothing like a deadline to focus you. And the focusing, like the obstacles that we talked about earlier, tends to spark lots of creativity, too.

I spend a lot of time planning. And I mean A LOT. It makes things easier for me. I then just get on and follow the plan through, and tick my beloved tick boxes.

This is F**k It in action: adapting your careful plan, mid-plan.

Though there's one thing I am good at, and it's essential to my planning abilities – I adapt the plan as I go along. A plan, a schedule, a budget, has to be flexible. I alter my plans and budgets all the time, based on how things are going: how long things are actually taking; circumstances that I didn't foresee; what I'm most enjoying doing, etc. And this, again, is F**k It in action: adapting your careful plan, mid-plan.

Follow the passion, not the plan

The plan can be so important for keeping us on track, and achieving the difficult task of implementation, but its very benefit (of keeping us on track) can be its problem too (in that the track might not be right for us).

So learn to follow the passion. If there's a scrap between the plan and the passion, let the passion win. Sure, once passion has won, you can recruit another plan to help make that passion part of your life, but the moment the passion 'moves on' (and the nature of 'passion' is to keep moving, so it *will* move on), dump the plan, and find a new one later.

Go implement

'A good plan violently executed now is better than a perfect plan executed next week.'

<small>GENERAL GEORGE PATTON – US ARMY OFFICER</small>

General Patton, who led US troops in World War I and II, was an early 'F**kiteer'.

Don't spend all your time planning, and never getting on with it. Implement your plan, even if it's not perfect. Even if it's not completely ready. Even if you're not completely sure. It's time to get moving. Actually, implementing what you've dreamed up, and what you've planned, is very difficult (well, it is for many people, me included, though some rare souls do find it easy).

It's difficult for a variety of reasons. A notable one is that we're probably scared: this is the ultimate test, after all. We can dream all we want about amazing ideas (oh, what fun), but there's no testing of those ideas. And we can plan all we want how to make these amazing ideas happen (oh, what fun), but there's no testing of those ideas.

F**K IT, I WILL MAKE THIS HAPPEN.

*This F**k It Push Mantra: Please do. The world needs it.*

But then there's the implementation (oh, what hell), which is all about testing. You're taking your precious idea to market. People have the chance to embrace it (aka 'buy it') or reject it (aka 'not buy it'). And no one likes the exam. In fact, no one likes the revision either. Bad analogy.

The thing is, even if you find the implementation stage difficult, if you can say F**k It and get on with it, then, when it works, it's an incredible feeling. To be tested and to succeed is better than not to be tested and not to know in the end.

Go get help, if necessary

So I find the implementation stage the most difficult. A lot of people do. Have a think now about which stages of this process you found (and find) easy, and which stages difficult. It's very good to understand what feels most natural to you – and where things just flow. It allows you to be gentle on yourself with the bits that aren't so natural – or to get help.

I find the ideas stage, and the planning stage, easy. But, as implementation is more difficult for me, it's the first area I should look at if I think I could do with help. And I do. Take this book, for example: though I have 'implemented' the ideas into the form of a manuscript full of words pretty successfully, and with relative ease, I won't have to implement the 'get the manuscript into the form of a physical book and then out into the bookshops around the world' stage. Hay House, my publisher, will do that. Thank goodness. I wouldn't be good at it. And I don't want to do it.

F**K IT, I NEED HELP.

*This F**k It Push Mantra: We all need help. This mantra helps you admit it and is thus your first step towards getting that help.*

Sussing out where your 'flow' is, then – in the whole process of manifesting a life where you're doing what you love – is very important. When you've understood it, you either take care in your non-flow areas, or you simply don't do it (if you can somehow get away with it), or you get someone else to do it. This takes a lot of F**k It: to keep going back to what feels right for you, and then rigorously delegating or discarding the rest.

If you'd like help with understanding where your flow is, you can check out a great system, 'Wealth Dynamics', which was developed by Roger Hamilton. On our website, www. thefuckitlife.com/dowhatyoulove, you'll find a link to a special online test you can take.

> *It takes a lot of F**k It to keep going back to what feels right for you.*

TURNING YOUR MONEY-EARNING VENTURE INTO A SUCCESS

Success rarely comes easily, and when it does: a. give thanks, b. ride the wave. The little guide that follows, though, will increase your chances of turning your venture into a success by something to the power of quite a lot.

Choose your battlefield

Clearly, there are a variety of ways to achieve success in business, but to keep it simple:

* **You could intend to be *better* than the others**. People started buying Japanese cars because they thought they were more reliable. People started buying Swedish cars (i.e. Volvo) because they thought they were safer. Whether they actually were or not is another matter. What really matters is perception.

    Stella Artois was probably no better than most other lagers, but it *was* more expensive (reassuringly so), so we assumed it was better. You could imply the superior quality of your thing by charging more for it (you kill at least two birds with one stone there, as your margins will be higher and your brand trust will be higher).

* **Or you could be *cheaper* than the others.** There are a million examples, but look at what the sports retailer Sports Direct have done in the UK. Though I live in Italy, I still wait until I'm in the UK to buy trainers, tracksuits and rucksacks in a Sports Direct branch because it's just so cheap.

   So the idea here is that you choose a market and you undercut the rest. These battlefields are bloody: just look at what's happening in the supermarket sector in Europe – with the German supermarkets LIDL and ALDI entering many countries with a much cheaper offer on a more limited range. So, unless you're willing to get your hands dirty, don't compete on price.

* **Or you could be *different*.** Create your own market. Or do something familiar in a completely different way. Some of the biggest brands on the planet have done things differently. Richard Branson's various Virgin brands have always done things differently. Branson would inject his own values into the brands to create this difference – whether it was a David vs Goliath quality (as with Virgin Airlines against British Airways), or transparent and authentic (as he did with Virgin Money), or being 'of the people' (as he was trying to do with his UK lottery project).

And while we're on the subject of battlefields, Richard Branson has always set his brands up against something: you can imagine him asking every time, 'Who's the enemy here? Who are we fighting?' He wanted to be *different* compared to the big corporates, or the money-grabbing banks, or the inefficient cartels. I imagine he would ask, 'What are we *not?*' as much as 'What are we?'

And then there's the biggest brand on the planet – Apple. Apple sets itself apart from its competition, as *different*, in many ways. The essence of the brand – that unique 'Apple-ness' – was created over years in many ways, but think how we tend to see Apple as somehow anti-establishment (even though it's the biggest company, the most profitable company, the market leader… it IS the establishment).

F**k It is different to anything else in the areas of spirituality and therapy.

Or how we see Apple as the cool, 'alternative' choice, the brand that early adopters choose (everyone has an iPhone these days, though, so how can that be the cool, alternative choice?). Or how we sense that Apple is somehow more egalitarian, more open, more inclusive than other companies (even though Apple products have a wall round them, so you can't use them with other systems, or other devices, and the company would turn away, embarrassed, if you mentioned the words 'open source').

In many ways, Apple's brand *appearance* is entirely at odds with the reality. Some of their kit might be *better* than their competitors, but even when it's not, they manage to charge about twice as much for it. Not only that, but people queue up overnight to buy the slightly different, newer version of something they already have in their pockets. This is the power of difference. And the power of a brand. You can make your own rules, spin your own myths, even set your own prices. You have some pretty titanic examples of how this can work.

The F**k It philosophy is *different* to anything else in the areas of spirituality and therapy. We have always stood out. It's not something we think about much, but we're so different that it's hard to know who we're competing with (as understanding your competition is usually a key element of building business success). So we tend just to get on and do our own thing, in our own way.

F**K IT, I'M HAPPY BEING DIFFERENT.

*This F**k It Push Mantra: Different is better than better. So 'happy' you should be.*

Choose your system

Choose the system you'll use to achieve the success you're after. And that will usually mean creating a *profitable* system. Choose how you're going to increase your margins:

* Is it because of a higher price than your competitors, due to your superiority or difference (real or perceived)?

* Is it because your costs are lower (maybe you're using cheaper labour, or you achieve scale, or you find a technology that can reduce costs)?

* Or is it because you're simply in an uninhabited market and you can do what you want?

Once you've created a system that works you can then grow it, by either hiring more people, or having other people run it, or automating it. Why? Because to increase success, at least in terms of money flow, you usually need to be able to UPSCALE.

You can think about this money flow as a river: to get more water-money through your river you can either increase the width or the depth of the river. The width could be the price: you could be in a market where your increased success means you could charge more – if you're a coach, for example.

If your business is entirely dependent on your own time (and is thus limited, income-wise) this is your only mode of expansion. This is why good lawyers, or doctors, or consultants, charge a lot – and keep on charging more… it's the only way to increase money flow within their system.

The depth of the river, then, is one way to scale up your unit production without requiring more of your time. The obvious way to do this is to hire people who are cheaper than you are to do the job you've been doing. Or, traditionally, you could get machines to do it. That's what the Industrial Revolution was all about after all: we moved from the cottage industry system (literally, individuals in their own homes with a loom each), to factories full of cheaper labour and loom-machines. The unit cost went down so the margins increased. And Marx and Engels had a field day noting the results.

Today, your bank's customer service department in India is not so far from the same principles: a combination of cheaper labour and machines (the automated 'press 1 for…' system; the cheap redirecting of phone calls; the instant access to vast amounts of information online – about you, your account, and the services you might want).

Now, the 'machine' is 'automation' in all its guises. Today, I could have bought a travel guide to Paris on Amazon, where I'd have had trouble getting to speak to a real person; I booked a flight and a hotel on my phone, with Ryanair and Booking.com, where again I'd have been lucky to talk to a real person. I checked the balance of my bank account online, as it's the weekend and they won't talk to me even if they could.

Automation reduces costs, increases margins, and thus increases the flow of money because of that depth increase. It can also, of course, increase frustration for everyone who's driven mad by automated phone systems. (And that, of course, creates another gap in the market – for companies that are happy to talk to their customers. This is a gap that the UK's First Direct bank has been exploiting for years.)

And it would, of course, be possible to automate much of what we offer in the world of F**k It. One example of an automated product that already exists is our 'F**k It Everyday'. The product is an inspiring F**k It message that's sent to you every day for a full year (see www.thefuckitlife.com/dowhatyoulove for details).

With automation, you can go to bed and still earn money.

But do you think I write a new message every day and send it out to you personally? No, of course not. I spent a long time writing and editing the 365 messages, then a longer time setting up the automated system to send those messages out. Yes, it took me a long time. But once it was done, it was done. Now the whole process is automatic.

The only manual element is that I receive (rather beautiful) emails from people saying how much they love the message of that day, and how astonishingly relevant the messages are, which is a testament to the magic of the machine, too.

With an automated system like that, once your initial work is done, then you're done. You can go to bed and still earn money. And don't people love the idea of that? Going to bed and still earning money (without being a prostitute).

That's a glimpse into the wonderful world of 'passive' incomes (though, as I mentioned earlier, very few incomes are entirely passive). Passive incomes have been around forever. Even before the biggest bestseller of all time – *The Bible* – was written. Have you ever wondered why you don't see God around so much these days? It's because he retired long ago into his gated community of Heaven, all on the back of the ongoing royalties from that master tome.

So, choose your system, and develop it so your margins are good. And, if you want, so that it doesn't depend on the number of hours that you do. One of the greatest systems ever invented was the franchising system largely attributed to Ray Kroc and his 'McDonald's' – he effectively took the factory mass-production idea and applied it to restaurants: McDonald's is the Model T Ford of the restaurant world.

Choose your metrics

If you're interested in the success of your business, how do you measure that success, and what do you measure along the way to get to that success?

Remember we used to run our retreat centre, The Hill That Breathes? The Hill was the mother of the whole F**k It thing. I'll take you down a few paths that demonstrate the metrics we used for that business. Clearly, the primary influence on our overall turnover was the number of people who booked a retreat. So we'd track bookings carefully. We knew that if we wanted to be full, we needed x advance bookings in January, y in February, and so on. If we missed a target one month, we'd have to try harder the next month.

And what did 'try harder' mean? Well, the obvious thing was the conversion percentage: how many of the enquiries we received were converted into bookings? What was that percentage? That was a critical figure, because, without doing any extra advertising or mailouts or social media activity, we could increase the number of bookings by upping that percentage. And we'd do that by improving the way we dealt with enquiries, or chasing people who didn't book straight away, or by making an offer to them.

> ## The Hill was the mother of the whole F**k It thing.

But, even with a high conversion percentage (our best has always been about 75 per cent, which means that three out of every four people who enquired about a retreat, booked), if we didn't have enough people enquiring, we were still not getting the bookings. We needed people turning up and looking at our site. Google analytics can give you a whole range of figures about who's looking, where they've come from and how long they stay, etc.

So for us, it was worth knowing what proportion of our enquiries were visitors looking at the retreats 'calendar'. And then seeing what proportion of the total visits to the site those calendar-viewers were. If we then made some tweaks to the site, we could see whether those proportions changed. And it's then good to see how any marketing activity affects these site visitor numbers.

So we had a variety of metrics for social media: as well as total number of fans, we'd look at total impressions, number of likes, etc. We could then easily track what would happen when we made different posts. Or, if we made an offer on a retreat, how that would then affect visitor numbers to the site, and the calendar, and the number of enquiries. So, if a critical part of 'success' for us was total number of retreat guests, then we had a whole range of metrics to help us keep those numbers high.

But businesses, clearly, are not just about turnover: they're about profits. So, you'll need a whole range of metrics that allow you to keep your profits up. You'll need to keep an eye on costs, of course. And it's worth knowing where your profits are actually made.

In a restaurant, for example, it may well be that most of the profits are made on the wine. So, getting people to sit down in your restaurant is important (that's the 'bookings' figure we were looking at), but it's whether they drink wine, and which wines they choose, that will most affect your profits. When my family and I go to restaurants, we often drink just water (and maybe a fizzy drink we can share) – so we've got used to the barely disguised disappointment of the waiting staff, as they remove the wine glasses from our table.

You'll need a whole range of metrics to help you keep your profits up.

But, you're wondering, what metrics can be used around wine consumption, and what can we do to affect these? Well, as well as measuring what proportion of diners order wine, and how much wine they order, you could measure how much they spend, on average, on a bottle of wine. If you're using all these metrics, you can start to play:

*   Do more people order wine if you fill your front window with wine bottles? (Passers-by will think, *Ah, this is a restaurant where you drink wine.*)

*   Do more people order wine if you drop the wine menu on the table before the food menu?

*   Does the type of food you provide affect wine purchases? Why not add wine suggestions to your main menu features?

*   What about leaving a bottle of (unopened) wine on the table? What about giving people a taste of one of your wines as an aperitif?

    *   What about the profit margins on the different wines?

There's a whole art (and science) to pricing that many large companies use – supermarkets are masters of this art – but small businesses often have no idea about it. For example, a high-end fashion retailer like Prada might put a £3,000 handbag in the window of its stores, but then have their £2,000 handbags inside the store.

When you see a beautiful £2,000 handbag, having just seen one at £3,000, your perception of that price has been altered. Yes, no

> **If playing price games feels manipulative to you, F**k It, don't do it.**

matter how crazy it might sound to someone like me, who'd never spend £2,000 on something like a handbag, if I've just seen one for the even crazier price of £3,000, it's still 'cheaper'.

Thus, by the way you price things, and the way you place your products, you can 'direct' people's purchasing. A supermarket will very carefully price a range of products, knowing that most people won't buy the most expensive items (cheapskates!) and they're also unlikely to buy the cheapest: they'll be buying the mid-price items.

So back to your wine. It's possible to 'direct' people's purchases by creating a sufficient range of prices. People will generally choose a bottle of wine from the mid-price range. Then you could ensure you have a higher profit margin on the mid-price wines. Clearly the mid-price wines need to be 'better' wines that the cheaper wines (though who knows how your wholesaler is pricing them to you). But they might be costing you £2 more, and you're charging £5 more for them.

If this all seems too manipulative for you, then, F**k It, don't do it. Add what you feel is a fair margin on top of what you buy the wine for. That's what most people do. But those that are making serious profits are playing the price games I've just been describing.

F**K IT, I WON'T DO WHAT I DON'T WANT TO DO.

*This F**k It Push Mantra: This is as important as doing what you do want to do.*

One thing about small businesses is that there's usually not much between struggling to break even, and making a nice little profit. Someone told me once about the owners of a chip shop who'd serve up a portion of chips, and, just before they wrapped it up (probably not in the previous day's newspaper, as they did when I was a kid), they'd take out one chip and pop it back in the oil.

That chip, they would say, was their summer holiday. You see? The difference between breaking even, and not being able to afford a summer holiday, and making enough profit to afford that holiday is… a chip! Remember the chip.

Your metrics, what you choose to measure, therefore allow you to assess whether you're on track to success, AND they give you a ready-made glimpse into the whole world of ideas that allows you to increase that success. Just measuring your business, in one way or another, will increase your success. And I've calculated, through an extensive range of metrics, that this is true in 96 per cent of cases.

Choose your role

The classic problem with Doing What You Love in business is that, sooner or later, you'll end up doing a whole range of stuff that you don't love. Especially, ironically, if you're successful.

So let's say that, when you were looking at what you loved, two things really stood out – that you adore making cupcakes, and that you love Louise Hay's affirmations: you love taking an affirmation card each morning and carrying that affirmation round in your head, letting its positivity reverberate through your daily life.

So you have an idea. You will make cupcakes with affirmations on top, artfully inscribed in piped icing sugar. People will then choose their cupcake based on the affirmation that most resonates with them. What a great idea.

So you start. You love the time you spend making the cupcakes and choosing an affirmation, and being with your friends (because your first customers are mainly your friends) as they choose the cupcake for them. A local café hears about your cupcakes and makes a regular order. And soon you're earning enough to be able to give up your day job. You couldn't be happier: you're doing what you love and making a living from it.

Before long, it's going really, really well. An article about your cupcake business in a big magazine results in an extra 60 emails in one day. New orders are coming in all the time. Regular orders. And you're struggling to keep up: to manage to make all the cupcakes by hand, as well as delivering them, and handle new orders, and answer emails, and issue the invoices. You're now doing all the business side during the day, and making cupcakes by night. Sometimes you're up until 3 a.m., inscribing affirmations on your cupcakes.

You're exhausted. It's not so much fun any more, and you realize you need help. Your sister's also a bit of a cupcake fan, so you ask her to help you. She makes the cupcakes while you look after the ever-increasing list of customers. Sure, you still choose the affirmations to go on the cupcakes, but your sister is now doing the very laborious job of making and decorating the actual cupcakes.

This eases the pressure for a while, and you breathe a bit more easily. It also gives you time to concentrate on the customers. Yes, some of those individual customers and friends, but also the bigger restaurants and shops that are making some really big orders now. It allows you to deal with their demands and, wow, don't they demand?! They have become very fussy about little inconsistencies on the cupcakes, and are now suggesting their own (rather awful) affirmations – and, if you're late delivering, they're very rude and threaten to cut the order.

A small business is like a dot-to-dot drawing – predictable.

I could go on. A small business is like a dot-to-dot drawing. You can probably fill the other dots in yourself. With most of those drawings you can actually see the image without filling in the dots, can't you? In other words, it's predictable. Most small businesses go this way. Well, if they're successful that is. The sad truth is that many small businesses fail and don't get the chance to experience this predictable path.

Because if making affirmation cupcakes for a living is what you want to do, and you do well with it, then you need to understand when to say 'no'. You will need to turn orders away. Or maybe you like the idea of running the business side of things. Maybe you're happy for someone else to make the cupcakes whilst you do other things.

You need, then, to Choose Your Role. What do you really want to do? What are you willing to do? Are you happy to switch roles as you go along? Or do you just want to do your thing? It's extremely important to understand what you're really after, because if you're not clear on it, everyone else will start to dictate it to you. And that's like going back to square one, isn't it?

Most of us got into the mess of not doing what we love in the first place by listening to what other people wanted of us, or suggested we should do, or thought we were good at. How many talented people are promoted beyond their original talent (and love) and spend their days in (management) misery? Don't let that happen again. If you're not clear about what you want to do, and where the limits are, then the world will dictate your role, and limits, to you.

I don't want you to be picking up this book again, in two or three years' time, exhausted and depressed, trying – again – to say F**k It and get back to Doing What You Love.

Choose your level of success

Because the success of your venture will affect your role so profoundly, it's worth anticipating what different levels of success would mean to you.

Most of us simply want to make as much of a success out of something as we can. It's apparently a very positive and abundant approach – to reach for the stars. It's an assumption within our culture now that we should all reach for the stars. Because who can doubt what it's like, once you're up with the stars? It's the dream: everything is beautiful, and touched with gold.

And if you truly want the highest success for yourself – and you're willing to take the downsides with the upsides – then that unswerving focus will take you far. But if you're more concerned about having a balanced life, or being able simply to do the 'thing' that you've found that you love, then Choose Your Level Of Success. Because there will be a point when the downsides of success outweigh the upsides.

" "

I said F**k It to my well-paid job as a lawyer and changed office desks for stages and business suits for yoga pants. I'm a yoga teacher and artist now. At the moment I don't earn much, but it feels as if I don't have to 'work' any more.

Instead, I can spend my days sharing my passion with lovely people, and that's just great. I will keep doing that for as long as it feels right for me!

SABINE HARBICH – VIENNA, AUSTRIA

" "

And, if we're talking about money, F**k It, how much (money) do you really *need* after all? Be careful of the trap of *for ever more*. There have been a few occasions in my life when I could have continued along a line that would have increased the money for ever more, and the success too, but the (non-monetary) price for that (monetary) gain outweighed the potential gain, so I said 'no'. And stopped. Be awake to those moments.

> *F**k It, how much (money) do you really need after all?*

Enough already

I remember the finance director of one company I worked for doing a presentation entitled 'Grow or Die'. As I sat there, I wondered whether that assertion really was true. But he certainly believed it, and the company invested hugely in growth. But it grew too quickly, and as the wage bill inexorably rose, the clients started to walk out the door, one by one. And the company only lasted a few more years.

I believe that company's rapid growth was a major contributor to its demise. And that's companies... We're probably not talking big companies in this book, are we? We're talking about you as a freelancer. Or you in a small business. But the pull to constant growth is still huge: if you can grow, then why not do it? If an opportunity arises, why not go for it?

But it's critical to recognize what is 'enough' for you. Especially if you value some balance in your life, and if you value continuing to Do What You Love. What is enough income? What are enough clients? What are enough working hours in the week? What is enough staff? What is enough success? What is enough fame?

All of the things that, in one way or another, denote success for us can be like drugs. We just want more; and even 'more' is never enough. I love the American expression 'enough already'. It's used to mean 'Stop, I've had enough of that'. You can use it to mentally mark the point and the moment when you have enough (of whatever) and don't need to do any more. Of course, if there's nothing you'd love more, then do more. But still learn to recognize that 'enough already' point.

For me, 'enough already' is the point on my balance sheet where the post-tax profits of our business are sufficient to give us a comfortable life (aka meals out, holidays, cinema trips, some nice clothes, etc.), plus a little bit to put aside for a rainy day. If I get to earn anything above that then the question 'Do you love this?' has to have an even better answer than usual – for example, 'Bloody hell, yes I do!'

Choose your means to upscale

Once you understand what you're happy to do, and what you're not, and what price you're willing to pay for various gains, you can say 'no' to various opportunities, and not expand. Or you can choose other means to upscale (or up-income).

You could increase your prices. If you double the prices of your affirmation cupcakes, say, you'll no doubt lose some orders, and the demand for them might drop. Maybe you'll lose half your customers. Maybe you'll have to make half the number of cupcakes now, for double the price. Maybe you'll make the same amount of money for half the work. Maybe you'll be back making the cupcakes yourself – which is what you've always wanted to do – and earning a good amount for this work. You'll be happy. Job done.

However, increasing prices is something to which most people are very resistant. It might be about fear (that people will stop buying), or a sense of not 'deserving' that amount. When I'm coaching individuals and small businesses (I just looked back at that sentence and see that I wrote 'small individuals' by mistake – yes, I only coach small people… children and those under the height of my mother; it creates an interesting niche market), this is where we have some of the most interesting conversations.

I have one client who offers advice in the realm of internet marketing. He's brilliant in his area: he has a vast amount of experience and can make his clients a fortune. But he was charging about the same rate per hour as a massage therapist. Not that a massage therapist couldn't be charging high rates per hour, but my client could have been charging three or four times more than he was, and his clients (the new ones at least) wouldn't have batted an eyelid.

In fact, I suspect that the advice he was giving would have been taken more seriously, and would have been implemented more readily (and therefore have had more of a successful effect), had he charged more for it. And that would have led to more clients – to the point where he would have been too busy, and therefore forced to increase his rates even more. But he was very reluctant to increase his prices. After some persuasion, he doubled his hourly rate for new clients. And everyone still said 'Yes, okay' without blinking. We're currently talking about how he could double the rates again.

Other ways to upscale? You could, in one way or another, automate an increase in your supply. This was done at the beginning of the Industrial Revolution by using machines to do the work that people had previously done. More recently, it was done in the car industry by using robots to do what people had previously done. And now, digital technology can perform a huge range of tasks that were once performed by people.

I've mentioned the boom in digital information products already. But, even with physical products, digital automation is transforming the market. You can do everything from your own tablet or phone. We used to sell our own F**k It T-shirts. We'd create a design (after driving for one hour to sit with our designer); send the design to a T-shirt company, who would print a couple of hundred shirts of different sizes, and send them to us. We'd then get orders (sure, online, with online payments), but we had to pack up the shirts and go to the post office to send them off to people. It was a lot of work.

This is what I did this year: I created a new design with our designer on Skype (which took half an hour); I then went to the Spreadshirt website, chose a range of shirts and sweat tops that I liked the look of, and uploaded the JPG of our design

Passive income, the F**k It T-shirt way.

to those choices I'd made – so I was able to see instantly how our design looked on these shirts, and how they'd look once they were produced. I then had our web designer feature this 'shop window' on our site and sat back and waited.

When people saw that shop window, and bought a T-shirt, their order was processed by Spreadshirt. They'd take the money, they'd print (on demand) the shirt, they'd pack it up and send it to the purchaser. And, at the end of the month, they pop the payment for each shirt into my Paypal account. Nice. I don't have to do a thing now. Passive income, the F**k It T-shirt way.

TURNING YOUR SUCCESS INTO SOMETHING YOU LOVE

That heading may seem weird. Haven't we based this whole thing on doing what we love? Wasn't that the bloody point? Well, you may well not want to read this now, but, in my experience, when we start off with something we love, all too often it ends up as something we don't. This is why:

* **We're dragged away from what we love** because of the demands of the business. I've mentioned Choosing Your Role and Your Level Of Success, but when this happens you

often have to make some tough decisions in order to get back to what you love, or to return to loving what you do.

I've realized a few things for myself in this area:

* a) as there will always be things that I don't particularly love alongside the ones I do really love, I've learned to be present to these things (to learn, in one way or another, to love them).

* b) my challenge is often about my overall workload. When I've less work overall, I'm happier with the overall mix: yes, doing things that I wouldn't normally enjoy, but also having the space to enjoy what I loved in the first place.

* c) at times, I've simply stepped back and stopped doing the things I don't want to do, and accepted the consequences.

* **We stop loving the thing we first loved.** It happens. Maybe we get bored doing it a lot more of the time: its joy was in the 'hobby' quality of it. Maybe the whole business side of this taints the thing itself – the 'Saul effect'. Maybe we get the thing out of our system. This has happened to me, to a certain extent, with the music. I will return to music, but I fulfilled so many of my desires around the music that, for now, the compulsion to make music every day has gone. I'm cool with that. Things change. My compulsions are elsewhere (currently on this book).

This is why it's best not to invest everything (emotionally, financially, reputationally) in your 'thing'. Saying F**k It is about being bold and making some leaps. But it's also about staying flexible, staying open, in every moment, to what you really love, and letting go when necessary.

The adventure of doing what we love

In previous F**k It books I talked about the *quality* of relaxation. That in the parsing of relaxation, the verb is more important than the noun… So, it's realizing that we don't just relax and then achieve a permanent state of relaxation. Instead, we are always in the *process* – the *verb* – of relaxing. That's the idea.

And it's the same here – with Doing What We Love. We don't go through a process of finding what we love, saying F**k It and doing it, and then we're there, in Happy Doing What I Love Land forever. Wouldn't that be lovely? But it's just not like that. Just as we need to be constantly aware of our state and our tensions when relaxing, and then relax through that, we need to be constantly aware of what we're enjoying and what we're not, and make the necessary adjustments or responses.

F**k It, you're unlikely to end up living in Happy Doing What I Love Land forever.

By combining 'Loving What We Do' with 'Doing What We Love', we turn this pursuit of a 'promised land' into a real and present and live adventure. It's not easy. Even (and sometimes, especially when) you're successful.

The tradition in this F**k It' book is to start a chapter with a quotation, but this time we'll end all this talk about how to make money from doing what you love with the words of someone who really knows how to make money: Richard Branson.

'I never went into business to make money – but I have found that, if I have fun, the money will come.'

CONCLUSION:
DON'T GO TO THE GRAVE WITH
YOUR SONG STILL IN YOU

*'Most men lead lives of quiet desperation and
go to the grave with the song still in them.'*
HENRY DAVID THOREAU, CIVIL DISOBEDIENCE AND OTHER ESSAYS

When I was writing about 'purpose' in Chapter 4, 'Do What You Love', I mentioned that I feel, experience, and live by, something different from 'purpose', and that's 'compulsion'. I've felt compelled to write this book for many years, and I've been planning it and working on parts of it for longer than my other books.

> **If I have a 'song' in this life, then F**k It is a great title for it.**

This book feels very important. I've felt that responsibility over the past few months as I've got down to writing the detail of it. I feel that responsibility now. If I have a 'song' in this life – some things I have to say in the style that I say it – then *F**k It* is a great title for that song; well, the whole album of songs actually. This particular *F**k It* song, *F**k It – Do What You Love*, is one that I've really needed to sing. Because I'm aware that so many people need to hear it.

F**K IT, I WILL SING MY SONG.

*This F**k It Push Mantra: If we can be arsed, we'll turn some of these F**k It Push Mantras into real embroideries. And this will be one of the first we do. Ladies and gentlemen, let's sing our songs.*

I don't know why this subject of Doing What You Love seems so *needed* right now, but it does. I was talking about Doing What You Love, and teaching some of the ideas in this book, years ago on retreats and weekends. But it's only recently, when I've mentioned it to participants on the retreats, and talked about some of the ideas, that I've noticed a kind of *hunger* for it. It seems that more and more people are realizing they have a song, and they need to sing it. Before it's too late.

I said F**k It and moved out of London, where I've lived all my life, and bought my dream cottage in the countryside. I've been here for eight months and I LOVE LOVE LOVE it!

Looking back, I should have done this some years ago; I don't know what held me back. Now I've said F**k It to my job in London; I've been doing it for 12 years, but it hasn't been working for me for the past four years. I'm about to start a new job locally, and I'm really excited. It's less money and more hours, but my peace of mind and welfare are taken care of. No more commute, no more stress. My exodus out of London is now complete. F**k It, what next?

TRACY LLOYD-EVANS – NOT LONDON, UK

Follow your compulsion

The peculiar quality of this subject means that my heightened sense of responsibility is inversely proportional to my ability to make it happen for you. In my other books, I've been able to say: 'If you do this meditation you will feel better.' And you do. Or I'll say: 'F**k It, realize that things don't matter so much, and feel the anxiety reduce.' And you do. 'Do this, after me, and you'll feel better.' And you do. It's 'Simon says F**k It'.

But with this Do What You Love subject, it's much more down to you. There's no formula that says, 'If you're not happy with what you do at work, leave your job, and try to Do What You Love.' Relaxing and breathing more deeply will make you happier. A + B = C. But leaving your job and trying to Do What You Love could end up in many places. A + B = X, where X is an unknown variable.

And that's the difference: there are so many variables here. Every situation is different. Each of you is different. Even the way in which 'what you love' works is different for all of you. Some of you might love the same thing consistently, no matter how much of it you do, for the rest of your life – whether it's painting or cooking or making money or gardening or teaching a foreign language. Others will find that, once they finally start to Do What You Love for longer than an hour, it bores them.

That's why it's important to 'Live By Doing What You Love': life is in a constant flow, we're in a constant flow, and what we love is likely to be in a constant flow, so we need a *stance* in life that recognizes that. A stance that's soft and flexible and constantly flowing itself.

And when the *compulsion* is there to move and to flow and to change, then we follow it. Both in the physical (and energetic) practice that we learned, and in life. In fact, that compulsion is a series of compulsions: compulsion flowing into compulsion as moments flow into moments. The flexibility of our *bodies*, and the flexibility of our *lives*, in response to that compulsion – which is dictated in both cases by the openness of our *minds* – is the dominant factor in how much we end up doing what we love.

And when we add simple presence and mindfulness to this compulsion-responding process – the secret ingredient – then we catalyse a magical dance between loving what we do, whatever we do, and doing what we love.

I hope this book contains most parts of the map that can assist you in whichever direction the compulsion leads you. And I hope it also has adequate answers to the numerous 'Yes, buts' that arise when we're faced by our own compulsion.

F**k It will help every step of the way. Whether it's the F**k It of giving up on something and letting go (maybe a career that you've been gripping on to for dear life, although it hasn't worked). Or the F**k It of summoning up the blood and stiffening the sinews that's required to make some big creation happen in this world.

When the compulsion is there, use Fk It to follow through on it.**

In *F**k It Therapy* I talked about the ability of F**k It to give a sense of perspective to our lives that we normally only get when we receive bad news (someone close to us dying, or being ill ourselves, for example). When we're faced with bad news, we ask: 'Well, why on earth was I worrying about *that* for so long? It really wasn't that important.' F**k It can give us that awareness and perspective on a daily basis, without the bad news.

In this book, F**k It has a similar ability: but this time it can help create a sense of *urgency* as well as *perspective*. And that's why I love that word 'compulsion'. If we can get into contact with that compulsion, and feel the urgency, then we can use F**k It to follow through on that compulsion.

And, again, we might only ordinarily get this sense of compulsion and urgency in the face of bad news.

> *F**k It can create a sense of urgency as well as perspective.*

A year ago, I was struck by a headline in *The Guardian* newspaper which read: 'Dying to Make the Most of Life'. The article itself was about a group of terminally ill people who had featured in a TV documentary made by the UK's Channel 4. They had all made radical decisions in the face of the knowledge that they weren't going to live for as long as they had thought.

In the article, Ann Munro, a palliative care psychotherapist who works with the terminally ill, said, 'Being told your future is limited focuses the mind in a way that nothing else can; and the tragedy is that it takes something this appalling to happen before a person ends up living the life they really wanted to live.' A terminal diagnosis brings implicit urgency, and the accompanying compulsions.

It is our opportunity – your opportunity, and my opportunity – to make contact with our compulsions every single day, and to follow them with a similar urgency, with the help of F**k It. Let's all do what we love more, every day. Let's love what we do more, every day. And let's initiate that dance between 'loving' and 'doing' that ultimately affects and creates our 'being'.

THE ONE-PAGE APPENDIX

Actually, this could be pretty much a one-line appendix, as I've put all the links to useful stuff on one page of our website, which is:

www.thefuckitlife.com/dowhatyoulove

But, so you know, you'll find the following there:

* The 'How F**k It Are You?' quiz.

* A link to 'F**k It Everyday', where you can get 14 days of F**k It emails for free.

* A song or two of 'F**k It Music'.

* Some lovely 'F**k It – Do What You Love' videos, and information about our 7-week course.

* The *F**k It, It Doesn't Matter So Much* e-book.

* Our free 'F**k It: Create a Digital Product' guide.

* The best guide to understanding what you're good at – a link to Roger Hamilton's 'Wealth Dynamics'.

* Links to the best people John knows in various areas, including digital marketing.

ABOUT THE AUTHOR

Gaia Pollini

John C. Parkin is the UK's bestselling wisdom teacher.

The son of Anglican preachers, John realized that saying F**k It was as powerful as all the Eastern spiritual practices he'd been studying for 20 years. Having said F**k It to a top job in London, he escaped to Italy with his wife, Gaia, and their twin boys, where they now teach their famous F**k It Retreats in various spectacular locations (such as on the volcano of Stromboli). He spends his days spreading the F**k It message – on the retreats, in F**k It eCourses and even with F**k It Music – then says F**k It himself and naps by the pool.

www.thefuckitlife.com

DO WHAT YOU LOVE WITH JOHN'S HELP

This book is just the beginning. And John can help you along the way with a 'F**k It – Do What You Love' retreat in Italy, regular eCourses and a high-level 'mastermind' group where you'll receive personal guidance from John and his team.

LIVE THE F**K IT LIFE

273

JOIN THE F**K IT AUTHORS IN PERSON IN ITALY FOR A F**K IT RETREAT

This is where it all started: John & Gaia ran their first F**k It Retreat in 2005.
They run these famous retreats in spectacular locations around Italy, including on the live volcano of Stromboli, on the beach of Pesaro and in a luxury spa near Urbino.
John now also teaches a 'F**k It – Do What You Love' retreat.
*Say F**k It and treat yourself to a F**k It Retreat.*

'Anything that helps you let go is okay on a F**k It Retreat.' THE OBSERVER
'I witnessed some remarkable transformations during my F**k It Retreat.' KINDRED SPIRIT

LIVE THE F**K IT LIFE

275

JOIN THE F**K IT AUTHORS ONLINE FOR A F**K IT E-COURSE

John & Gaia have a range of F**k It eCourses available, including John's new
'F**k It – Do What You Love' 7-week course.
So you can say 'F**k It' and explore the F**k It teaching in depth from anywhere
in the world.

Printed in the United States
by Baker & Taylor Publisher Services